To Brandon

When I was a kid,
there was a moment that changed my life forever.

My Dad gave me my first hockey stick.
It was my introduction to the sport
that taught me so much.

At first, I didn't want to even pick it up
because I didn't want it to break.
Once I picked it up, I never wanted to put it down…

Every stick I owned started out looking pristine but the more it
broke down, the more lessons I learned.

With all the grinding in practice and in games, I soon learned that
the stick was not the most important piece to the puzzle.

It was the tools between my ears and in my chest that mattered
the most!

Grampa Bob
2021

TABLE OF CONTENTS

PREFACE

INTRODUCTION

1) CHAMPIONS DO THE WORK

2) DO MORE THAN YOUR TEAMMATES

3) VISUALIZATION

4) TAKE THE EXTRA STEP

5) RESPECT YOUR LEADER

6) LOOK AROUND

7) DRESSING ROOM PREP

8) EAT WELL TO PERFORM

9) RESPOND DON'T REACT

10) MOTIVATION>DISCIPLINE>LIFESTYLE

11) START PLANNING TO BECOME GREAT

12) 40% RULE

13) SELF-TALK

14) OPEN THE DOOR

15) FAILURE IS NOT TRYING

16) LEARN EACH DAY

17) CROSBY FACE-OFF STORY

18) ANY GIVEN DAY

19) ALWAYS BE THE UNDERDOG
20) WHAT DRIVES YOU
21) WHO IS YOUR HERO
22) YOU 10 YEARS FROM NOW
23) BLOCK THE SHOT
24) MAKE YOUR BED
25) I AM GOOD ENOUGH
26) PASS THE PUCK
27) BE RESILIENT
28) NEVER GIVE UP
29) ASK FOR ADVICE
30) ROLE MODEL
31) PAST DOESN'T DEFINE YOU
32) PERFORMANCE VS POTENTIAL
33) HOW BAD DO YOU WANT IT
34) FAIL TO PLAN, PLAN TO FAIL
35) INTERNAL FORTITUDE
36) HOW HARD HAVE YOU REALLY TRIED
37) SAVE THE MONEY
38) LITTLE DETAILS MATTER
39) YOU NEED TO SEE TO BELIEVE
40) DRINK THE WATER
41) DARE TO COMPARE
42) PICK THEM UP
43) BUILD THE TEAM
44) TRUTH MAY HURT

45) STUDY AND STUDY SOME MORE
46) TREAT IT LIKE SCHOOL
47) THE PHONE IS A TOOL
48) HOLD YOURSELF ACCOUNTABLE
49) ACCOUNTABILITY COACH
50) GET SOME SLEEP
51) VALUE YOUR SUCCESS
52) QUALITY VS QUANTITY
53) WHO IS WATCHING
54) FLY, SWIM, GROW
55) HABIT OVERHAUL
56) BE A DREAMER
57) BE THE DIFFERENCE MAKER
58) PROVE YOURSELF
59) HAVE FUN
60) DO IT RIGHT THE FIRST TIME
61) GRIT IS FREE
62) CHANGE YOUR MIND
63) BENCH YOUR EGO
64) ACCEPT YOURSELF
65) BE RESPECTFUL
66) THE BULLY
67) STAY IN THE MOMENT
68) STOP COMPLAINING
69) IT'S OK TO BE BORED
70) WINNERS DON'T MAKE EXCUSES

71) KEEP CHIPPING AWAY

72) DISCIPLINE NOW

73) OLD SCHOOL ROAD HOCKEY

74) BUY A STOPWATCH

75) OLD SCHOOL MINI-HOCKEY

76) READ THE COMPETITION

77) PRE-GAME MOVEMENT

78) PROS GO TO WORK

79) DON'T JUST MAINTAIN IT

80) WON'T ALWAYS BE PRETTY

81) KEEP ROLLING

82) PAY YOUR DUES

83) TAKE THE CHANCE

84) BELIEVE IN THE END RESULT

85) BACK TO THE BASICS

86) YOU ARE THE BEST

87) IT'S THE LAST 10%

88) SIZE OF THE DOG

89) DON'T BE NERVOUS

90) YOU HAVE CONTROL

91) ARE YOU SCARED TO SUCCEED

92) FANCY FOOTWORK

93) HILL TIME

94) GRAB A PIECE OF PAPER

95) YOU NEED A BREAK

96) IT GOES BOTH WAYS

97) STOP JAW JACKING

98) YOU DON'T NEED 10 MOVES

99) CLIMB THE MOUNTAIN

100) THE REWARD

Conclusion

Bonus: How to Plan Your Perfect Day

Additional Resources

PREFACE

I have had the opportunity to work with many young athletes over the years.

There have been so many amazing moments and memories created.

There is one story that I found really impressive and would like to share some of it with you.

This young man started playing ice hockey at only 5 years old and fell so in love with the sport that he decided he wanted nothing more than to become a better hockey player so he could eventually play in college.

He became interested and asked many questions to why his parents always went to the gym….

He snuck in rides on his parents' exercise bike…

He practiced agility drills on his skates and performed many off-ice skill drills.

He ran up and down hills with his dad in the forest.

He went to the local track with his dad and pushed sleds and did lots of sprints.

He didn't quit and never lost hope!

Now, only 12 years old at the time of writing this, he finally made the AAA Youth Hockey Team in his city.

This team is regarded as the highest level team for minor hockey in our area.

It's quite the accomplishment for any young man to be on the roster.

But what I found even more impressive is that he got cut 3 times from the AAA team and twice by the AA team before he got accepted to the AAA hockey team!

To show that much determination as such a young man was inspiring and thought provoking to me.

What was responsible for this young man's fierce determination? I just had to know?

I approached this 12-year-old boy and asked him the burning questions on my mind.

When I finally asked him what he thought was most important along this journey, this is what he told me.

paraphrasing

There are always two voices in my head.

One voice always tells me why I CAN'T do something.

You're too tired to work out. Stay in bed.

You're too small to make the hockey team. Stop working so hard for it.

You will get cut again, so why keep going?

But the other voice always tells me why I CAN do something, ya know?

I know you're tired today, but you've still gotta get your workout in.

You're smaller than almost all the other kids on the hockey team. That just means you're going to work that much harder and try to outwork everyone on the ice!

You have to continue to work on your weaknesses, improve your skills even on the days when you don't feel like it.

I was taken back by the profoundness in this boy. He was only 12 years old, and in my opinion, had already stumbled across one of the greatest human discoveries made to date.

Let me explain…

If you go back through history and observe any culture that has ever existed, they too talk about two sides within themselves.

A dyad of good and evil.

In Japan, people would look to the sky and write stories of good luck dragons that would dance across the clouds, embodying the characteristics many people strived to have…

…but also tell stories of being haunted by Oni (evil spirits) that seemed to amplify the negative aspects of people's character when they were around.

In China, they had Yin, a white koi fish associated with lighter emotions and good fortune in the world…

…and Yang, a black koi fish associated with darker emotions and unfortunate natural phenomena in the world.

In ancient Greek mythology, there was Zeus, king of Olympus and a pure representation of power and worship…

…and his brother Hades, king of the Underworld and a representation of darkness and fear.

And my personal favorite is the Native American tale known as "The Tale of Two Wolves."

In this tale, a young boy approaches the medicine man in the village with questions about the world.

"Why do bad things happen?" asks the boy of the medicine man.

With a chuckle, the medicine man replies…

"Inside each of us there are two wolves.

One wolf is white and stands for things in the world like joy, love, happiness, excitement, wonder, and gratitude.

The other wolf is black and stands for things in the world like selfishness, greed, anger, hate, and lust."

In awe of the medicine man's story, the young boy asks, *"Which wolf wins?"*

Smiling again, the medicine man says, *"The one you feed."*

I find these stories from different cultures fascinating because almost all of them have observed and documented the same discovery this young man had made.

There are two voices inside all of us.

One inner voice that encourages us to be more, be better, and achieve what we really want in life…

…and one voice that will always try to talk us out of accomplishing our dreams.

This is called a dyad (something that consists of two opposite parts).

And every human has a dyad of good and evil, inspiration and discouragement, toughness and weakness.

This is not a bad thing. In fact, I believe that having a dyad in ourselves is one of the great human gifts we have been blessed with.

But…

In today's society, it seems we have forgotten that we have this dyad within ourselves.

We are told that if something hurts, or something is not fun for us, or the voice in our head tries to tell us we shouldn't be doing this…

…it is suddenly a "bad" thing for us to pursue.

This is where I disagree with modern culture. And I believe that ancient cultures of people throughout history would also disagree with where we have found ourselves as a society.

Instead of shying away from things that may be uncomfortable in the moment...

...I believe pursuing something that may be uncomfortable can actually bring profound POSITIVE consequences to our lives.

Let's just observe a few examples of great people who have endured great unpleasantness to achieve greatness.

Wayne Gretzky

As a huge hockey fan, I have to start by talking about the greatest hockey player ever, Wayne Gretzky.

Born and raised in Brantford, Ontario, Wayne developed an obsession with hockey as a young man.

Never being the tallest, fastest, or strongest player on the ice, Wayne had to find other ways to dominate the hockey rink.

This led to countless hours of Wayne playing imaginary games in a backyard hockey rink alone.

He would zip back and forth across the ice, narrowly avoiding clips from imaginary players and slapping shots home...

He would sit behind the opposite team's goal and brainstorm creative ways to score from unique angles...

And he would play images in his head over and over again of him leading his team to victory...

Throughout most of his early hockey career, Wayne would spend hours alone on the ice, just picturing the moments when he would lead his team to victory.

His teammates and friends would go party night after night, but Wayne was diligent in his practice year after year.

Eventually he became the world's greatest hockey player and led his team to four Stanley Cups.

But it all started with his backyard solo hockey games.

Kobe Bryant

It is no secret that Kobe is known as one of the hardest working basketball players of all time.

Just listen to this story from Kobe's teammate Ryan Celestand.

"The first time I began to understand why he [Kobe] was the best was in the preseason. In a game against the Wizards, Kobe broke the wrist on his shooting hand. He was always the first person to practice every day, arriving at least an hour and a half early. This would infuriate me because I wanted to be the first person to practice, just as I had always been at Villanova and Piscataway High in New Jersey. To add insult to injury, I lived only 10 minutes from the practice facility — while Kobe was at least 35 minutes away.

"I am ashamed to say that I was excited the day after his injury because I knew that there was no way that No. 8 (as former Laker point guard Tyronn Lue called him) would be the first to practice, if he would even be there at all.

"As I walked through the training room, I became stricken with fear when I heard a ball bouncing. No, no, it couldn't be! Yes it could. Kobe was already in a full sweat with a cast on his right arm and dribbling and shooting with his left."

This voracious work ethic allowed Kobe to go onto win five NBA championships with the Lakers and made him debatably the best player to ever touch a basketball.

Kobe employed what he called the "Mamba Mentality." This concept is based on one having mental fortitude and extreme focus and relentlessness during practice and competition!

R.I.P. Kobe!

Oprah winfrey

Before her famous talk show, Oprah was told she was, "not fit for television" by one of her higher-ups at the beginning of her career.

Instead of giving up, Oprah doubled down and became even more determined to make it on TV.

She had come from a life of poverty with her mother, and her father had taught her toughness.

It was months later when Oprah was contacted to potentially host a talk show that went on to be named simply "The Oprah Winfrey Show."

Oprah's show is now quite possibly the most well-known and successful talk show in America, maybe even the world.

And she only has this show because she refused to listen to so-called "professionals" in the TV business. Instead, she listened to the voice inside her soul and kept going.

Oprah was what we call a "Underdog."

You may feel like you don't have what it takes and that no one believes that you will accomplish great things.

It is never too late, and you are destined for greatness.

Oprah took that first step, but more importantly she never stopped moving until she accomplished her grand goal!

Colonel Sanders

The founder of KFC spent most of his life struggling to get by without any real direction.

When he retired at 65, Sanders committed to his secret chicken recipe and made an effort to franchise his new company, KFC, across the country.

He started his venture at 65, so you must believe that wherever you are right now, it is not too late to accomplish your deepest and wildest dreams!

It wasn't until Sanders was 73 years old (eight years after his retirement) that he finally sold KFC for 2 million dollars and signed a contract to remain the face of the company.

By 88 years old, the Colonel was a billionaire.

Most people would retire and try to live out the rest of their life without working, but the Colonel was different. He was not satisfied with a simple retirement. He wanted more.

So, he spent the first eight years of his retirement starting a business that would eventually make him over a billion dollars.

Each of these people above had many moments in their careers when they could hear the voice in their head screaming at them...

"GIVE UP! You'll never make it!"

But every one of these people drowned out the dark voice in their head and chose to listen to a brighter influence that was quietly murmuring encouragement to them from deep down.

By listening to the brighter voice in their soul, these people were able to accomplish extraordinary things that most people would have thought impossible.

And it all started with just a tiny minor accomplishment that gave them the confidence to continue listening to that bright voice in their head.

So let's bring this back to the wisdom this young 12-yearold hockey player was kind enough to share with me.

After telling me about the two voices in his head, I asked him if he thought his life was going to be different in the future because he had made the AAA hockey team.

Would he continue playing hockey?

Would he pursue something else?

I was curious.

He went on to tell me that college hockey was his dream for now. But knowing that he was able to make his AAA hockey team gave him the confidence to know that he would be able to accomplish anything in his life.

It could be hockey…or maybe something entirely different.

Regardless of where life leads him, his confidence in him-self from making the AAA hockey team has poured over into every other area of his life. There is no doubt in his mind that he will be able to succeed at whatever he does with enough hard work.

And there's good news…

This confidence that this young man has is something that anybody can possess.

Accomplishing ONE THING can give you the confidence you need to go on to accomplish anything else in your life IF you want it bad enough.

There is an art to achievement, and that is what you will learn in reading this book.

What you'll find in the pages that follow are pieces of advice I've picked up from working with dozens of young athletes, millionaire business coaches, and bright young minds that are just getting started on accomplishing something phenomenal.

Because I grew up playing hockey, and my own son is now following in my footsteps of really enjoying hockey as well, the content that follows will quite often come back to…well, hockey lol.

But the purpose of this content is not only to teach you to become a better hockey player…

It's something much bigger than that.

What lies in the pages ahead is a formula for success in almost ANYTHING you do that I call "The Art of Achievement."

It is a handbook for resilience. And a bible for those committed to creating success in their life through determination.

My hope is that you will use this book to strengthen the bright voice inside of you so that you always have the encouragement and belief that…

You Can Accomplish ANYTHING.

INTRODUCTION

Remember this…

You are NOT being graded for reading this book.

You don't have to finish it.

You don't have to turn it in.

You are reading this book for you and you only.

While most typical schooling "punishes" you with poor grades or a stern lecture…there are no negative consequences for you if you do not read this book.

But there is missed opportunity…

The older you get, the more you will have to choose carefully where you invest your time.

Right now, you may be spending your time at school, on sports, homework, and then trying to relax or hang out with friends in the little time that you have left over.

That's GREAT. I mean it.

This book should not prevent you from living your life or missing out on fun times with your friends.

First and foremost, education is your number one priority. You never know how the cards will fall with regard to sports but one thing is certain: no one can ever take your education away from you!

Whether you are in the classroom, hockey arena, or somewhere else, there are always so many opportunities to learn.

Do not hide in the back of the class!!

Be the kid in the front row who raises their hand because they want to learn and grow.

I am not just talking about the school classroom. Learning opportunities are everywhere if you are willing to ask and open your mind to the endless possibilities.

I can tell you that the books I've read and the people I've learned from in my free time have changed my life on a daily and fundamental level.

Because of the choices I made to invest in myself OUTSIDE of typical education, I have been able to change my life and people's lives around me. And it all started with deciding that I wanted MORE than a typical education.

I know I can't tell you what to do (nor do I want to), but if I may be so bold as to give you a tiny piece of advice…invest in your own education now, inside and outside the classroom. It will help more than you know as you get older.

This book is not only a hockey book, it's a compilation of the lessons I've learned that I wish I knew when I was playing minor hockey.

Now, my hope is that these same lessons can help you as well.

As you read through the following chapters, remember what I told you in the beginning of this book.

You do not have to read this book.

But if you do…know that you are consciously choosing to become a better hockey player, leader, and person.

And when you make enough choices to become better than you "have" to be…you become a person with the power to change the world for the better.

In the following pages, you will encounter *100 Ways To Unleash Your Hockey Potential*!

You will not be able to accomplish them all at once but greatness always begins with the "first step."

Start today, choose a category below, and get moving, because your dreams must be non-negotiable.

There will be days when you don't feel like it, and the easier route would be to skip your training session.

There will be times when the progress seems non-existent, so the next step would be to take it easy and let your guard down or maybe even quit!

From this day forward, remove the word "quit" from your vocabulary and replace it with "grit"!

To live the life of your dreams, you must never quit!

Your dreams are too important to leave up to chance, so let's begin with one ground rule, once you identify a "goal," you must assign a date to it and write it on a calendar!

Now you have a trackable timeline to complete the assigned tasks along the way to achieving your larger goal.

Finally, not everything will go as planned, and the goal may seem unreachable.

Do not stop and compromise your dreams. The goal must stay the same, but the path to the goal may need to be altered and adjusted.

Once you begin your journey, you must keep moving and maintain that forward momentum, and whatever you do, do not quit.

All dreams are achievable, if you want it bad enough!

To your future success.

1
CHAMPIONS DO THE WORK

Are you the type of player who only does the minimum work that was assigned?

Do you just complete the prescribed drills because that is what was asked of you?

People who aspire to be champions have come to the realization that just completing the "required" work is not going to be enough!

Your performance will be indicative of how you practiced, so if you are cutting corners in practice, it will be exposed in the games!

So, what do champions do that average players do not?

These action steps must become part of you moving forward!

ACTION STEPS

1) Champions do NOT stop one foot short of the line when doing skating drills.

2) Champions DO extra off-ice drills when no one is watching.

3) Champions put their FULL EFFORT into their schoolwork.

4) Champions DO the extra repetition or skate the extra foot.

5) Champions outwork their competition.

6) Champions Never Quit

7) Champions are Leaders.

8) Champions will Fail and Learn

9) Champions Have Grit.

10) Champions all started somewhere!

I'LL DO THE WORK!

2
DO MORE THAN YOUR TEAMMATES

Be honest with yourself, how do your teammates view you?

Are your actions in practice, off-ice, and during games aligned with those of a respectable teammate?

You may be thinking, "I don't care what people think, I am my own person and will act how I want!"

Absolutely, you must be true to yourself and not be constantly trying to keep other people happy.

You can DO BOTH!

Currently, are you the type of player that is inspiring all your teammates or are you just another butt on the bench?

The opportunity for inspiration begins in practice, and here is how you do it!

You MUST outwork your teammates every practice. WHAT? Isn't that self-serving?

Kind of, but not really….

View your teammates as competition during those tough skating drills and make the decision that you will not lose a race again!

Here's what happens when you decide to adapt this attitude:

1) You become better because you aspire to be the hardest worker on the

ice.

2) By treating each drill as competition, you are building resiliency. When times get tough late in a game, you are ready, because you have been competing when everyone else is just going through the motions of the drill from practice.

3) Your teammates' performance will improve as well because you continue to raise the bar. Nobody likes to look bad in front of their teammates. They aren't just going to let you beat them in every drill. So, when you treat the drills like competition, they will too. Your practice intensity will increase and everyone begins training at a higher level.

ACTION STEPS

1) It all needs to begin somewhere. WHY NOT WITH YOU!!

2) Where do you rank on your team in respect to the hardest workers?

   Who works harder than you?

3) It's time to increase your intensity and become the hardest worker on the team!

LEAD FROM THE FRONT!

3
VISUALIZATION

What is visualization and have you even tried it?

Does visualization sound weird and only done by strange people?

Give me the puck, and I will dangle everyone and snipe it top shelf!!

That's what hockey is all about, right? Skating, Shooting and Scoring!

Have you heard of Wayne Gretzky?

Gretzky is the leading scorer of all time with 894 goals, 1,963 assists, totaling 2,857 points.

Wayne Gretzky and many other elite athletes believe in and would recommend that all athletes should be doing visualization techniques.

Ok great, but how do I even get started, and when do I visualize?

You can practice visualization anywhere; just close your eyes and envision what you would like to come TRUE!

However, this technique is something that you cannot just do once and have everything you want become reality.

Download your big goal into your brain; see it and feel it!

No, it won't be handed to you just because you are thinking about it. This coupled with relentless pursuit and hard work will help you reach your goals faster.

To increase their effectiveness, it is beneficial to practice visualization techniques on a regular basis.

A great time to do this is on the car ride to the arena, in the dressing room before the game, and even just before you go to sleep at night.

Start slow and keep it simple!

Here are some suggestions for you, covering all the positions in hockey.

ACTION STEPS

HOW TO DO IT:

Take 5 minutes each day and visualize your desired outcome!!!

Below are some examples based on hockey positions.

1) **Goalies** - Visualize yourself making that big save during crucial moments in the game. Picture yourself catching the puck, sliding across the crease to make the save, the crowd cheering, and teammates patting you on the back!

2) **Defense** - Envision yourself reading the play and stepping up to steal the puck.

   Picture yourself winning those defensive battles in the corner and in front of the net. Visualize making that lead pass to a forward and them streaking in to score the game-winning goal!

3) **Forwards** - Are you a play maker or goal scorer?

   If you are a play maker, close your eyes and visualize yourself making that pass to a teammate. Gretzky was a magician from behind the net. Visualize yourself feathering passes from behind the goal. Goal scorers must picture themselves scoring during a puck battle in front or sniping goals using their wicked shot!

   Your brain is a powerful tool. Use it wisely.

   If you want something to happen bad enough, start visualizing it in your mind, like it's already happened.

   The best part....IT IS FREE!

YOU MUST SEE IT FIRST!

4
TAKE THE EXTRA STEP

Are you a relentless backchecker?

If someone beats you, are you willing to catch them and alter their shot at all costs?

Often we think that it's the player who scores the goal that is our most valuable player.

I would rather have players on the team who DO NOT QUIT and backcheck like their lives depended on it, rather than a player who scores some fancy goals!

"How do I become an amazing backchecker, I'm not that fast??" you might ask.

There are many fast players in the game, but are they willing to push through the burning lungs and heavy legs to save the game by lifting the opponent's stick?

It's what is inside that counts, that burning desire to stop the opponent, no matter what.

Let's get started, so you will be a feared opponent!

Do not just compete, it's time to dominate!

ACTION STEPS

1) It is now your mission that the other team will not score when you are on the ice.

2) Picture the other team scoring because you decided to not take a few extra strides and lift the opponent's stick. How does that feel, knowing your decision to quit was the difference on the scoreboard?

3) Visualize yourself as a backchecking machine!

4) *Be the difference maker!* If you are consistently skating hard back into your end and saving goals, your teammates will take notice and these attributes will soon be adopted by those around you.

DEMAND MORE FROM YOURSELF!

5
RESPECT YOUR LEADER

When is the last time that you approached your COACH and asked them

"How can I improve?"

Why don't you?

Are you worried about what they will say?

A great coach will offer you feedback on the areas of your game that need improvement.

A great player will listen intently and not argue or get offended. If you try to defend yourself, you will limit the necessary truth needed to improve your game.

If you get your back up, you are signaling to the coach that you are really not that interested in their feedback.

Great players are on a mission to be the best, and they seek feedback because they know it will lead to more and more growth opportunities.

Ever heard of Michael Jordan…the greatest basketball player of all time?

You may also have heard the story of how he got cut from his high school team, but there was much more to that story.

Jordan had the talent to make that team, but his attitude was terrible and his coached called him out on it and released him.

Jordan knew he was skilled and questioned the coach's decision.

Here's the best part!!

The coach said to him, "If you want to make my team, your attitude needs a lot of work." He then advised him that he would like to meet with Jordan every day before school to work on his game.

Michael Jordan met with this coach every day before school, put in the work, got outside his comfort zone, and developed the skills that were once his deficiencies.

If he didn't accept his coach's advice, would we have ever heard of AIR JORDAN?

ACTION STEPS

1) Communicate with your coaches; they are there to help.

    Do not be offended or try to defend your ego.

2) If you are in a development program, ask your instructor where you can improve. The more quality feedback you can receive, the more doors for personal growth will open for you.

    It may not seem like it, but there are so many people in this world who just want to help, if you are willing to listen!

    GET THE FEEDBACK AND THEN DO THE WORK!

6
LOOK AROUND

Have you ever heard of the term "situational awareness"?

High performing players have excellent situational awareness!

Situational awareness is very important but often overlooked for the more common components in hockey such as skating, shooting, and passing.

Do you focus on where the puck is or are you surveying the other areas of the ice?

Being super aware is knowing what is going on away from the puck and anticipating what is going to happen next.

Example: Your teammate is putting pressure on the defenseman. Is it smart to just charge into the corner to help them out?

Instead, read the play! Are they going to throw the puck up the boards or pass it cross ice?

Sidney Crosby has unbelievable situational awareness. He is consistently reading plays, deflecting, and even intercepting passes!

I once attended a game in Detroit where Crosby had a significant impact every time he was on the ice.

It was unbelievable how he saw the ice and anticipated what was going to happen next. I pointed this out to my son, and he didn't find it that exciting because there was not a goal right away.

Crosby intercepted passes, altered the passing lane and deflected many opposing passes. All of these actions prevented the opposing team from moving closer to the Penguins' zone.

Crosby was not the leader on the score sheet that day. However, I deemed him the MVP because every single time he was on the ice, he had a direct impact!

ACTION STEPS

1) Be aware and start looking around the ice more. When you do not have the puck, start anticipating where the puck will go next. Then you will be a step ahead of the rest!

2) Do not just watch the game when you are the bench. This is a time to learn and read the play.

3) Look up videos of Crosby and study his situational awareness techniques.

BE AWARE OF YOUR SURROUNDINGS!

7
DRESSING ROOM PREP

Are you focused and prepared before the game?

We all know those players who mess around before games.

They are not focused, and when the game begins, they are not mentally prepared.

There will always be players like this on our teams. They are talking about a video game or a Tik Tok video that has no bearing on the game that you will be playing.

It's often limitations from other people that affect our potential.

Are there teammates or people in your life that are limiting your greatness?

If you want to perform at a higher level and continue to improve, you must limit your time with the troublemakers.

When you are getting dressed for the game, you are putting on your uniform for battle.

Flip the switch and stay focused on the task at hand.

ACTION STEPS

1) Job Roles - Think about what your main job roles are on your team.
2) Visualization - Close your eyes and envision what you will do in the game.

3) Flip the Switch - What you say to yourself is a very powerful tool.

4) Pre-Game Routine - Do you have a game day routine?

Many professionals have the same meal on game days. They don't just show up at the rink and play the game.

How are you preparing at home? Are you hydrated and eating healthy? Did you sit around all day or get the blood moving?

What are you focusing on when you are driving to the arena?

Where is your head at in the dressing room?

Is the teammate beside you focusing on the game too or distracting you from the task at hand?

You have potential but if there is no "planning," the potential is limited!

HANG WITH THE RIGHT CROWD

8
EAT WELL TO PERFORM

Do you pay attention to the types of foods you are putting into your body?

This is not a nutrition book, so let's keep it simple and easy for you.

Nutrition is often overlooked because when you are young, you may be able to eat whatever you want and your body always looks the same.

Just because your body looks the same on the outside, it does not mean it is operating efficiently on the inside.

The food that you put into your body is fuel. Proper nutrition provides you with the opportunity to train harder, longer, and recover more efficiently.

Your body is ready for another training session to help you move past the competition who continues to eat fast food all the time.

There is only one person who decides what food will go into your system and that is YOU!

Limit processed foods with multiple ingredients! Your body does not recognize this man-made processed garbage!

All NHL teams have a nutritionist that helps players choose appropriate food that helps them perform and recover more efficiently.

If the top players in the world understand the importance of nutrition, the decision to eat healthy should be a no-brainer for you!

ACTION STEPS

1) Eat natural foods. If you stick to the outer aisles in the grocery

store, you avoid the man-made processed garbage.

2) Food Sensitivities - The body uses specific foods better than others. Many people are sensitive to certain foods. This is not to say you are, but you must pay attention to how your body responds. How do you feel one hour after eating bread, pasta, or dairy-based foods?

Common Food Sensitivities:

**Gluten

**Dairy

If you feel sluggish, tired, and not energized, that food may not be your best fuel choice.

FEED THE MACHINE WISELY!

9
RESPOND DON'T REACT

When was the last time you acted out of emotion?

Did you slash someone because they tripped you?

Did you bang your stick on the ice because you thought the referee should have called a penalty?

Did you lose your cool after a loss and were disrespectful to the other team because you were mad?

If you have not done any of the above, you are either lying or you are the coolest, calmest, most collected player in the game.

How can you control your emotions in the heat of battle?

The first step is acceptance. There will be many things on and off the ice that are not in your control.

You cannot control if someone slashes you or if the referee misses a call.

You cannot control what someone says in a text or on social media.

However, you do have control over how you react or more importantly, how you will respond.

ACTION STEPS

1) You Will Lose - You will lose many games in your hockey career.

   Be respectful to the other team; they are hockey players just like you who love playing and put a lot of effort into it.

RESPOND - What will you do after the game? What effort will you put in so that you limit future heartache?

It sucks to lose, but if you "look" close enough, the answers are there...now it's up to you!

2) They Slashed Me! - You will get slashed, hacked, tripped, and punched if you play hockey long enough. If you react out of emotion each time, you may as well move your bed into the penalty box, because that will be your second home!

RESPOND - When you get slashed or hit, take a deep breath. The brain wants you to react and stand up for yourself. If you can wait a few seconds, you will have a much better chance at controlling your emotions and not "reacting."

If you react out of emotion, your team will be shorthanded and your poor decisions will inevitably effect your ice time and your happiness level!

There is ONE person who controls your emotions and that is, of course, YOU!

3) Meditation - If you have had instances where your patience was tested and you responded with anger, meditation would be a very good choice for you. Try it for 5 minutes each day.

It will help you control your emotions on and off the ice.

When Kobe Bryant entered the league, he was truly a student of the game and wanted to learn as much as possible to strengthen his game. During the NBA Finals, he watched intently as Michael Jordan and the Chicago Bulls maintained composure during the entire finals.

Their emotions remained the same, whether they were up 10 or down 10.

That is because they had an innovative coach named Phil Jackson. Jackson implemented meditation into the Bulls players' daily regimen.

Coach Jackson's coaching philosophies helped lead the Chicago Bulls to six championships!

You will remain in a more positive state throughout the game. Negative energy is not good for your performance and that energy will rub off on your teammates!

YOU HAVE THE CONTROL!

10
MOTIVATION>
DISCIPLINE>LIFESTYLE

Are there days when you feel motivated and ready to dominate?

Do you have moments when you do not feel like doing anything?

The words "motivation" and "discipline" are words that get used in sports time and time again.

However, LIFESTYLE is what you should be striving for!

Let's use an example in relation to running a hill to get in shape!

Hill running is great for cardiovascular and leg strength, both of which are important for hockey players.

"But, hill running is hard, and I don't really feel like doing it," you might think.

MOTIVATION - People can be motivated for a short period of time by getting pumped up from a song or video. Sometimes this will work, and you end up on the hill running.

DISCIPLINE - This is when you begin showing up and doing the work even when you don't feel like it. There will be times when you miss the workout because you were not motivated and disciplined enough to show up. That is human nature.

LIFESTYLE - This is where good players become GREAT PLAYERS.

When something becomes part of your lifestyle, it becomes non-negotiable.

This is "you" now!

It is your lifestyle that will put you in the position to surpass the competition.

**To increase the chances of making something part of your lifestyle, your goals must have deep meaning to you!

Your VISION must mean something to you! There is not a huge difference between successful and unsuccessful people.

Often the gap lies in their desire to reach their potential.

Do not sell yourself short.

Do not underestimate the power to dream big!

ACTION STEPS

1) Get out a piece of paper and write the word WHY at the top.

    Take a few minutes and think about what your big goal is.

    i) Is it to improve each year?

    ii) Is it to make a specific team?

    iii) Is it be the goal scorer or the best playmaker?

Now that you have established your MAIN GOAL, it becomes easier to complete tasks when you do not feel like it.

Do things that others won't, so you can have what others can't!

IT ALL STARTS SOMEWHERE!

11
START PLANNING TO BECOME GREAT

Have you spent a few minutes and established your BIG WHY?

Awesome, now let's put a plan in place to get you there! First, we begin with the GOAL.

Let's say that you decided that you want to make a higher-level team.

If you are to move up another level, you will need to improve in many areas of your game.

If you want to make vast improvements, you will need to get out of your comfort zone.

You will make mistakes and may feel like you are failing.

This is NOT TRUE. Failing is not trying in the first place.

Every step that you take outside of your comfort zone will provide opportunity for self-improvement.

THE PLAN

1) When is the date for the tryout for the new team?

2) Now, you plan backwards.

3) If there are 90 days left before the tryout, you have some work to do, but if you put in 100% effort, you will give yourself a much better chance.

4) So, what should I be doing for those 90 days?

5) Start by being honest with yourself! What areas of your game need work? Write them down. Now put them in order of importance. The #1 item is your highest priority and you must take action to begin improving this area.

EXAMPLE LIST

1) Skating

2) Edgework

3) Passing

4) Stickhandling

5) Cardiovascular

6) Strength

Now, to ensure that you improve in every area before tryouts, you must start scheduling them into your day and week.

Speak to your parents and explain your WHY and that you are committed to improving!

Ask them to book extra skating and edgework for you.

Now, #3-#6 are FREE!!

You can practice passing and stickhandling in your driveway or basement.

Start by scheduling in 5 minutes each day for passing and stickhandling. Then move it up to 10 minutes. You will be amazed at how quickly these skills will improve.

If you need assistance improving your cardio or strength, reach out to your parents for guidance. If you need further advice, consider speaking with a fitness coach.

Keep it simple!! The basics work and are effective. There is no secret sauce; if you are consistent each day and work on all the areas mentioned above, you will IMPROVE!

You may make the team, you may not. The most important thing is that you committed to something that means a lot to you. You put in the extra reps when no one was watching.

You built resiliency and adopted a "Never Give Up" attitude.

These skills will serve you well as a person, not just in hockey.

ACTION STEPS

1) Write out your WHY.

2) Make a list and prioritize what needs attention.

3) Commit to your schedule and book these activities into your daily plan.

GO GET IT!

12
40% RULE

When is the last time that you looked in the mirror and asked yourself, "Do you really put in 100%?"

At the end of practice, games, and the end of the day, only YOU know if you put forth YOUR BEST EFFORT!

The Navy Seals believe that your body can handle a lot more than we think we can.

They say that most people are only operating at 40% of the body's capabilities.

How do I reach my potential? What does that feel like?

When you take your helmet off, do have a sweaty head?

When you come to the bench after a shift, do have to sit down to catch your breath because you gave it your all?

Are you willing to take the two extra strides and catch the player before they take the shot?

Your body can handle all of these, but it's your mind that limits you from surpassing that 40% rule!

If you are willing to get uncomfortable, be exhausted after a shift and gassed after a game, success is right around the corner!

When you are consistently working outside your comfort zone, it is possible to start reaching levels higher than the 40% cap.

Dedication, grit, and determination will ensure that you can raise your level.

Just think: if your body is operating at 60%, 70%, or even higher, the competition will be left in your dust!

How do we know when we are at 40%, 50%, 60% or even higher?

Let's use an example from hockey practice.

Think back to the last time your coach said, "Get on the line and don't touch the pucks."

You skated and skated, gasping for air before your next turn.

You questioned whether the drill would ever end, and the more you thought about it, the worse it would become. A lot of people quit and throw in the towel because they don't know when the pain will end. Their brain will then rationalize that it's time to quit because there is no way you can keep doing this with no foreseeable end point.

When you start breaking the drill down or the shifts in the games down into chunks, you are capable of much more than you ever imagined!

Do not look ahead to how many more lines or circles you have to complete.

Focus on the "next one." Complete it to your best effort.

Then focus on the "next one." Your body is capable and will continue to complete the repetitions.

Once you begin to tackle practices and games this way, you will move past 40%, 50% and onward and upward!

ACTION STEPS

1) When you are tired, you must have a way to not let your mind win. When you think there is nothing left in the tank, say to yourself, "I don't get tired." Say it now 5 times...feel the energy that comes into your chest.

Use this strategy on the ice when your brain is telling you not to take those extra few steps.

Those two steps may be the difference in winning or losing the game!

MIND OVER MATTER!

13
SELF-TALK

How do you talk to yourself?

What, doesn't talking to yourself mean you are crazy?

Positive self-talk on and off the ice is another great tool for you to add to your Hockey Bag of Tools!

The 40% rule applies here, and if you want to move past 40% and get closer to 100%, you must overcome the limitations from your mind.

When you are doing skating drills in practice, start saying "I don't get tired!"

When you are tired at the end of a shift, say "I don't quit!"

Take that extra stride and make a difference.

Your brain is a very powerful tool if used wisely. Believing in yourself and building the self-confidence is so important.

When you start believing that you can be the best and that nobody can outwork you, success will follow.

You are good enough and it's time to unlock your potential.

Your biggest obstacle is YOURSELF!!

ACTION STEPS

1) Start recognizing any negative self-talk.
2) What are you saying to yourself. I can't, I won't, I'm tired, I'm

not fast, I suck.

STOP!!

Replace these with I CAN, I WILL, I MUST, I DON'T GET TIRED, I AM GREAT!!

3) Journaling - A daily journal or planner allows you to be aware of what may be working and what may not.

It allows you the opportunity to write down how you are feeling and what type of self-talk has been going on.

If you write these entries on a consistent basis, you will be able to review and analyze the positive and negative patterns.

You have GREATNESS within you. The first step towards greatness is YOU believing!

GO GET IT!

14
OPEN THE DOOR

When is the last time you held a door open for someone?

When you hold a door open for someone, what do they say to you?

They say, "Thank you!"

In the hockey world, there are many doors available to you.

Every door opened can lead to an opportunity!

Do not leave any door unturned!

What are you talking about???

Think of it this way…how many opportunities are you leaving on the table because you are fearful of being embarrassed?

Everyone makes mistakes. The room for growth is increased when we stop worrying about what other people think.

Be yourself!

Make it a commitment to learn, grow, and soak up what knowledge is available to you. Meet with loved ones, coaches, and friends and discover the holes in your game.

Success does not happen overnight, even though it may appear that way.

The champion was not always on the top; there were so many actions and steps that were completed behind the scenes.

ACTION STEPS

1) Raise your hand and ask the coach where you can improve. If you don't, you will never know!

   Do not take it personally and defend your current actions.

   Take their advice and improve in that area.

2) Do the Right Thing - If someone on your team makes a big mistake, it's your time to be the supporter. Many players may be angry at that player because they cost you the game, but you need to do what is right!

   How do you think they feel?

   Hit them on the pads and offer support.

   Other players may view you differently, but don't worry about it! It was the right thing to do!

   You are a great teammate during the highs and lows!

3) Sign up for a class or train with people above your current level. If you are training with players above your skill level, you will naturally improve and begin playing at a more advanced level.

SPRINT RACE EXAMPLE

If you are always the winner but never improve your time, you are not personally growing.

If you train with more advanced people, you may get last place, but you will consistently set new personal bests!

THE OPPOSITION IS THE OPPORTUNITY

15
FAILURE IS NOT TRYING

Are you afraid of failing?

Are you afraid of being embarrassed in front of other people?

We don't like to look inferior in front of other people, so often we will not even try!

Go back to your piece of paper with the WHY on top of it.

If you have not thought about what your big WHY is, stop and take a few minutes to establish your BIG GOAL!

Now that you have made it REAL, did you set your standard high enough?

If you set a goal that is not outside your comfort zone, you may never reach your full potential.

Everyone has the ability to accomplish their wildest dreams, so why don't we?

The common levels of fear are:

i) Fear of looking bad

ii) Fear of failure

iii) Fear of success

Have you ever completed a "Fears Exercise"?

Simply grab a piece of paper and write down your fears!

Are you fearful of being embarrassed?

Are you fearful of failing?

Are you fearful of succeeding?

SET A NICE AND BIG GOAL BECAUSE YOU DESERVE IT!

ACTION STEPS

1) Fail often! Get used to it, because if you do not fail, you will never reach your full potential.

2) At the end of each week, reflect on the past week. It is ok if things did not go as planned.

    Write down the areas that you did not succeed in. Now, schedule in time each day the following week to improve on these areas.

3) Learn from your failure! When you fail, you must view it as a learning experience.

    Did you fail because you are not quick, not strong, a poor shot, can't pass, or don't have a winning mindset?

    Each time you fail is a learning opportunity. People who accept failure as their reality will continue to operate below their full potential.

    Learn from your deficiencies and execute the plan to improve.

FAILING TO PLAN, IS PLANNING TO FAIL!

16
LEARN EACH DAY

Are you a student of the game or do you just show up and do the minimum?

Do you load up a YouTube video and learn from the best players in the world?

Have you ever asked your parents to buy you a book for Christmas instead of a video game?

This all comes back to your WHY!! When your WHY actually means something to you, it will be much easier to do the work necessary for improvement.

Learning something new each day is not meant to overwhelm you.

You do not have to learn a major skill. YouTube and books are offering you education directly from your idols, who are the best players in the world.

Do you already have a great hockey background and feel there is really nothing else to learn?

When you step back, humble yourself, and become vulnerable, you have just expanded the realm of learning!

There will always be opportunities to learn and get better if you are willing.

Here is an example of a simple yet powerful skill:

When you are skating into the corner, turn your head and look to see where everyone is on the ice. Now, when you pick the puck up, you have a general idea where your teammates are. You can make that pass to the player streaking in from the point! If you didn't turn your head, you may not have seen that opportunity!

ACTION STEPS

1) Use YouTube as a hockey resource.

2) Request a book not a video game.

3) Human connection - Knowledge is available everywhere.

Do something every day to improve your mindset and challenge yourself.

Read books, watch podcasts, take a course, speak to your coaches and mentors.

ASK QUESTIONS!!

BE THE STUDENT IN THE FRONT ROW!

17
CROSBY FACEOFF STORY

Do you perform the dirty reps behind the scenes?

Years ago, Crosby won a faceoff that led to a game-winning goal in the Stanley Cup Playoffs.

As his team lined up, he told the defenseman that after he won it back to him, he would go D to D for the shot. That is exactly how it happened, and they scored!!

That may not seem like much on the surface. It was just a faceoff, right?

Earlier that day, Crosby attended an optional practice and spent most of it working on faceoffs. This was not the only practice or time he spent on practicing faceoffs. He was relentless and wanted to become one of the best at taking faceoffs. He made it priority and didn't stop until the mission was accomplished.

He has always strived to fine tune the little details within his game and out-work his competition.

CHAMPIONS understand how many reps need to be completed if they are to perform at the highest level in sport!

Thousands and thousands of faceoffs behind the scenes to have the opportunity to win the *one* that counts.

Nobody is going to lie down and let you win that faceoff.

ACTION STEPS

1) Behind the scenes - Put your best effort in when nobody is

watching.

2) Identify the skill that will separate yourself from the pack.

Use your phone and record yourself Day 1. Day in, day out you will continue to fine tune your skills. Continue to record yourself to gauge your progression.

Study the progressions and study the mistakes so you do not make them over and over again.

3) The reps! It may seem like enough, but do you think Crosby ever says, "that's good enough?"

IT IS ALL WORTH IT!

18
ANY GIVEN DAY

How often have you thrown in the towel before the game even started?

"They are in first place, so we don't have a chance, do we?"

Have you ever seen the movie *Any Given Sunday*?

If you haven't, set aside some time and tune in.

The short story is that it doesn't matter what place you're in, any team can win at any given time!

Another great story you must check out is the *Miracle On Ice*!!

The USA Olympic hockey team pulled off one of the biggest upsets in sports history!

Remember, the other team is made up of kids just like you. They are the same age and put their pants on one leg at a time, just like you.

Don't write yourself off before the game because someone else tells you that you have no chance!

ACTION STEPS

1) Standings don't matter! When you are playing a team that is higher in the standings, be aware of how your team is acting.

    If you see that everyone is throwing in the towel before the action has begun, be a leader, stand up, and get them fired up!

    **This situation is actually a great opportunity for your team to come in and beat that first-place team. You are the underdog and no one is really giving you a chance, including the kids in the opposing dressing room!

2) Always a chance! You will always have a chance if you and your teammates put forth 100% effort.

HARD WORK IS MORE IMPORTANT THAN TALENT THAT DOESN'T WORK HARD!

19
ALWAYS BE THE UNDERDOG

Do you feel like an underdog, on the ice or off the ice?

Do you feel like people don't believe you can do it?

Here's the thing, you should always view yourself as the underdog!

Remember, any team can win on any given day, so why can't you be the next great success story?

Do not ever let anyone tell that you are not good enough!

All success stories begin somewhere, in a place where the person had to take the first step.

Where are you now?

What is your current skill level and what team do you play on?

The great thing about underdogs is that they have nothing to lose!!

People are not giving you a chance. They do not think you will make it, so if you are willing to put the work in each and every day, you are going to surprise a lot of people, especially yourself!

CHAMPION MINDSET

Your current performance level does not define who you are.

There are daily opportunities to improve, will you embrace them?

Champions will do the work behind the scenes when no one is watching.

Will you dig deep when no one even knows you are training?

Will you do it even though at the end, there will be no "good job" or a pat on the back?

Champions improve, slow and steady. They will be more than ready when they get their shot.

People think that they got lucky or they must have been super talented.

You know better. You did the work when you didn't want to but you did it because you BELIEVED in yourself when no one else did!

GO GET IT!

ACTION STEPS

1) Have the vision! Ensure you have a clear GOAL that you want to achieve.

    Spend 5 minutes daily visualizing yourself achieving that outcome!

2) Make a list of the things that you need to accomplish and establish a timeframe to complete them.

    Then you have the framework for your success path.

    **Schedule these items into your day. Pick an exact time when you will work on specific skills.

    When the dream is important, it becomes non-negotiable and much easier to show up and do the work!

3) Feel it and believe it deep inside your soul that it is time to show the world that you are ready to shine.

    Start turning some heads!! You are good enough! Keep showing up and do the work that most people are not willing to do!

UNDERDOGS HAVE THE ADVANTAGE!

20
WHAT DRIVES YOU

Are you self-motivated or do you need something to get you fired up?

You signed up to play a sport where you will be a winner some days and a loser the next.

There will be games that your team does not play well but still find a way to WIN.

There will be games that your team played great but somehow you LOSE.

There are moments in every game when you need to dig deep.

I'm not talking about digging deep physically; you will need to dig deep mentally to get through the obstacles.

How can you do this on a consistent basis even when you just don't feel like it?

MAKE IT EMOTIONAL

Early on in my hockey career, I got cut from a team, and I was devastated.

I didn't understand what happened, as I did very well on that same team the year before.

I knew one thing for sure and that was that I never wanted to feel like that ever again.

That day, I vowed to never get cut from another team.

Every practice, I aimed to be the hardest worker on the ice.

Every battle in every game, I adopted a "you will not beat me" attitude.

This strategy was only going to work if I was consistent. I couldn't just show up for a few practices or games and expect to continue playing at a high level.

This was a commitment I upheld throughout my years playing hockey.

I would refer to this as "flipping the switch," creating the mindset and work ethic that nobody will ever outwork me.

Your physical size can be an illusion to your potential. It is the size of your heart that really matters.

Grit, grit, and more grit!

I never got let go from another team!

ACTION STEPS

1) The hurt! Identify the moment in your life when you didn't get what you wanted and it hurt bad.

2) Use it to your advantage! That event now becomes FUEL. Every practice, every game, everything you do behind the scenes.

THE HURT IS NOW FUEL!

21
WHO IS YOUR HERO?

Think for a second, "Who is my hero?"

Really, think about it…who do you look up to and want to follow in their footsteps?

It could be a professional sports figure, a coach, a sibling, or it could be your parents!

It is important to look up to someone and start emulating their behavior.

They have reached high levels of success and that is what you are striving to do.

However, success should not be measured by the dollars in their bank account.

The money in the bank account may be a product of their success, but they had to do many things to acquire that status.

So are you wondering what the "recipe for success," shortcut is?

The shortcut is that there are no shortcuts.

All greats that you look up to have ONE THING in common!

They do not GIVE UP!

You may already be working really hard and feel that you should be in a better place than where you are now. Is it all worth it or should you slow down or maybe stop?

It's easy to feel defeated when we are going through tough times and there are more problems than solutions.

However, the hardships in your life will lead to something better, and often something that you may never have imagined could come true.

Stay with it every day and one thing is for certain, you must not stop!

Consistency = Success!!!

ACTION STEPS

1) Choose a hero.

   Study their daily habits.

   Write them down and begin scheduling them into your training plan!

2) You can have more than one!

   If you want to be great, begin doing the things that the greats are willing to do!

TIME TO BE GREAT!

22
YOU 10 YEARS FROM NOW

Have you ever viewed yourself as a hero?

Now that we have focused on how important it is to have a hero that you can learn from, I want you to also look at it in a different way.

Be the HERO in your own story!

You all have a story that you are writing each day.

You all deserve to have an amazing story!

This is not an easy feat because not every day is going to seem like positive momentum.

Each day, there will be many little decisions that you have to make and these decisions will in fact mold who you become 10 years from now.

Here is an example that will ensure you are on the path to creating the best version of yourself today, tomorrow, and certainly 10 years from now.

When performing tasks, there will be a point when you can continue or stop.

***When you are thinking about quitting, say "Remember tomorrow."

Think about how you would feel tomorrow if you quit.

There is much more honor in going all in and giving it all you've got and finding out it wasn't enough, rather than wondering "what if?"

So, how do we ensure that you have the story that you can be proud of?

ACTION STEPS

1) Picture yourself 10 years older, looking back at your current self.

    This helps with your daily actions on and off the ice. Would you, 10 years older, be proud of your current work ethic, study habits and respect for other people?

2) Start using this tactic. It helps you become accountable to yourself and the standard that an older "you" would be proud of.

YOU HAVE SO MUCH POTENTIAL!

23
BLOCK THE SHOT

Do you block enough shots?

Are you willing to get in front of the puck for your teammates?

Blocking a shot may hurt in the moment but you may have just blocked the game-winning goal!

In hockey, there are so many little details that get overlooked.

You have to be fast, strong, and have a wicked shot to be successful... don't you?

Sure, those are important but GRIT often gets a lot less coverage.

SIMPLE MATH

If you limit the number of shots taken on your goalie, your team has a higher probability of winning the game.

If all teammates blocked a few shots every game, that would be 30 less shots on your net!

Success will not always be fun and may hurt from time to time.

Years ago, the talented Edmonton Oilers could not beat the New York Islanders.

After they lost the Stanley Cup Final, the Oilers got undressed, upset but not very banged up.

A few of them walked by the Islanders' dressing room, and many of the players were dressed or half-dressed with ice packs on their bodies.

They were sore, banged up, but smiling ear to ear because they had won another championship.

They understood that discomfort was part of the process. The entire journey on and off the ice will have instances when you can take the easy road or the harder path.

The success and championships are waiting for you!

How bad do you want it?

ACTION STEPS

1) Don't turn your body. You do not have pads back there!

2) When you go to block the shot, try to get closer to the shooter so the puck won't be travelling as fast.

3) Be aware of what hand the shooters are on the ice.

    When you are setting up for the shot block, you will be more successful if you go towards their forehand.

4) When you are thinking about whether you should block the shot or not...look at it this way, you could be blocking the game-winning goal!

BE A TEAM PLAYER!

24
MAKE YOUR BED

Do you make your bed each and every day?

What?? I'm not reading a hockey book to hear that I should be making my bed every day!

My parents are already on me constantly to "make my bed!"

Hear me out.

When you make your bed, you are completing a task very early on in the day.

You have just started the day with an accomplishment, and you are now in a positive mindset!

You have begun the day with momentum and are more likely to continue that task-completing focus throughout the day.

If you start the day by checking social media (which is someone else's story), you are now saying to yourself that their story is more important than your success.

You are developing a positive habit. Successful habits breed successful people.

Are these habits part of your current lifestyle?

i) Healthy eating

ii) Quality sleep

iii) Continual learning on and off the ice

iv) Scheduling in your most important items into your day

v) Boundaries for social media time

Here is your morning recipe for success

ACTION STEPS

1) Wake up and make the bed first thing.

2) Drink some water.

3) Complete a skill that you need to work on. This could be as simple as going to the basement or garage and practice stick handling for 5-10 minutes.

4) Have a healthy breakfast.

There you go, you now have 4 WINS before you have even gone to school.

***Make It A Challenge

For the next 30 days, complete one item before you check your phone.

That could be to make your bed or choose a skill to work on!

**HOW YOU DO ANYTHING IS
HOW YOU DO EVERYTHING!**

25
I AM GOOD ENOUGH

How often do you think to yourself, "I am not good enough," "I can't compete at this level," or "I'm done"?

Think back to the last time that you said these things to yourself…try to remember where you were when you had these thoughts.

This is classified as negative self-talk and should be limited.

It will take time, but when you change that negative internal dialogue, you become the person that you are meant to be.

Maybe throughout your life, people have said things to you to make you believe that you are not good enough and do not deserve greatness.

Over time, we can start to believe this garbage, and we start to speak negatively to ourselves. We lose confidence and do not perform very well in many areas in our lives.

If you are feeling this, I know it hurts, but it will get better.

Tom Brady, arguably the greatest quarterback of all time, was drafted in the sixth round.

He was deemed weak, slow, and to not a very good throwing arm. To become an NFL quarterback, you would agree that those attributes were needed.

Brady continued to believe in himself. He was relentless and trained harder than ever and was a true "student of the game."

His consistent studies led him to be one of the best at reading defenses, which made his job much easier. He started recognizing what the defense was going to do and would capitalize and find the open receivers time and time again.

This sixth round draft pick has appeared in ten Super Bowls and has raised the trophy seven times, the most in NFL history.

Do not ever let anyone tell you that it cannot be done!

ACTION STEPS

1) Be aware! Begin recognizing your patterns of negative self-talk!

   Avoid the naysayers! Don't worry about what people are saying. They have their own issues, we all do.

2) Practice makes permanent - Embrace your journey, always learn and do not stop!

3) Practice positive self-talk! Greatness is inside of you.

   Begin speaking positively to yourself each day!

   Say, "I am great," "I believe," and the most important, "I DON'T QUIT!"

IT'S TIME TO BE GREAT!

26
PASS THE PUCK

On a scale of 1-10, how would you rate yourself as a play maker?

If your answer is below 8, you have some work to do!

Why do I need to pass the puck if I score 50 goals each year?

When you pass the puck to your teammates, you ironically will become an even better player and will have more opportunities to score!

Selfishness has no part in team sports and will hinder a team's success.

When players move away from self-serving, selfish behaviors, the TEAM will thrive!

BE A TEAM PLAYER

In life, the more you give back, the more it comes full circle back to you to reap the rewards.

In hockey, if you choose to be a selfish player and not pass the puck, your personal growth will suffer and the team's potential diminishes.

Wayne Gretzky is the all-time assist leader, and Sidney Crosby continues to find the open player before worrying about his own stats!

What do these two monumental players have in common?

THEY SEE THE ICE REALLY WELL AND MAKE EVERYONE ELSE AROUND THEM BETTER!

Many people have even said that they have eyes in the back of their head!

You may never reach the heights of Crosby or Gretzky, but it's never too late to sharpen your passing repertoire.

ACTION STEPS

1) Look around - Keep your head on a swivel and be aware of where everyone is on the ice. Not just your teammates. When you gain possession of the puck, there is limited amount of time to make the right play. If you know where the competition is, you will start making those passes to your teammates quicker and with more accuracy!

2) Practice - A lot of young players spend endless hours practicing their skating and shooting but very limited time working on their passing skills.

   Passing practice is FREE!

   If you want to become a great play maker, spend the time in the basement or driveway working on technique, efficiency, and forehand and backhand passes.

   Have fun with it and be creative.

   DON'T BE A SELFISH PERSON!

27
BE RESILIENT

Do you feel that everything in life should be handed to you just because you showed up and maybe did a little work?

Let's hope not, because as you move through the different levels of hockey and life, there will be many moments when you will not receive what you thought you should have.

The sooner you learn how to accept failure, the quicker you will be successful!

What…how does that make sense?

Each time that you fail is another opportunity for you to learn.

Close your eyes and think of a time when you felt like the outcome should have gone in your favor, but it didn't.

You have a choice at this point. You could roll over and just GIVE UP; let's hope you did not make that choice. Maybe you did, but it's not too late.

You could have blamed others. You could have felt bad for yourself and made the decision to stop working hard because it doesn't seem worth it.

Or, you can look at every failing moment as a great opportunity to learn.

When you didn't make a team or you didn't bury the game-winning goal, those are only blips on the radar of your life and potential.

Many people will not accept that losing is a part of life. They stop trying because of the heartache, and now they are miserable because of their unlived potential.

Do not be afraid to fail.

Failing is not trying in the first place!

ACTION STEPS

1) Fail to learn - The next time you fail, take a moment and assess what else could have been done to prevent that situation. Study the mistakes over and over. The mistakes may have even cost your team the game, which made you upset.

   Use this to get to work because you never want to feel that way again.

2) Skill refinement - Do you are having difficulty scoring from in close? Start practicing in close shots, dekes, and one timers. Keep it simple!

   Identify WHY you failed and spend some time on that area. Before long, your weakness will become your new strength!

FAILING IS NOT TRYING!

28
NEVER GIVE UP

Can you remember a moment when you know for sure you didn't put in 100% and failed?

Could you have back checked harder, passed the puck to the open player, or maybe you decided to not study enough and tanked your test?

But, this isn't a book about school, is it?

Well, the habits that you have away from the arena will help you become a better hockey player.

We have talked about what CHAMPIONS will do, especially when they do not feel like it.

They may feel great today, but there were many times when they didn't feel like putting in the extra hours of hard, sweaty repetitions, but they did anyway.

This is why they are great today!!

Back to the school example. If you are always cutting corners in the classroom, you will be more apt to cut corners in other areas of your life.

How you do anything is how you do everything!

When you attack each task in life with focus and your full 100%, you will be amazed at how your hockey game will improve.

"How does that work, I don't believe you!" you say.

When you make the decision in life that you will never give up, you have made the decision to be excellent. You are now holding yourself to a higher standard.

You may not always win, but at least you tried.

You won't succeed the first time, the second, or maybe even the tenth.

At this point, it may seem natural to say "I can't." This causes negative energy within yourself and can lead to self-doubt.

If you fail, try again. If you fall, get up. If you lose, learn from it!

Whatever you do, never give up!

ACTION STEPS

1) Every task! Give your best every time. That could be in making your bed, cleaning your room, how you treat people, how you study, your effort in hockey practice, your effort and attitude when things are not going your way.

2) Be a leader! - Lead by example and complete the task to the highest standard.

You will fail and fall down and it won't feel good.

Think about your deepest dreams and get up and finish what you started!

This behavior is contagious. Other people and teammates around you will start behaving like you and NEVER GIVE UP.

BE A BETTER PERSON, BE A BETTER PLAYER!

29
ASK FOR ADVICE

Are you the kid that sits in the front row at school and raises their hand and asks a question or do you hide in the back row?

Sometimes it is hard to raise your hand because you don't want to be singled out and feel embarrassed.

If you truly want to learn, you will have many questions, and people in this world will help, you just have to ASK!

Each time you make the decision to not raise your hand, you are limiting the opportunity to learn and move closer to your potential.

Sure, there will be people who never raise their hand in life or in the dressing room. That is reality, but it does not have to be your reality.

Get comfortable being uncomfortable! *This is where the growth occurs.*

When you receive the answers in the classroom and do the work, your knowledge base will increase, your grades will soar, and your confidence will rise!

On the ice, if you do not fully understand the drills being explained, raise your hand and ask what is expected of you.

When you understand the expectations and direction, your confidence will be higher.

When confidence rises, so does performance!

As confidence in your game rises, you will begin to trust yourself in situations where before you may have just "hid in the back row"!

ACTION STEPS

1) Start raising your hand!

   In the dressing room, on the bench, at home, and in the classroom.

   If this is something that you have never done, it won't be easy.

   If your END GOAL is meaningful, you owe it to yourself to take the first step and put your hand up.

   It will get easier after that first rep!

2) Do the work - When you receive the answer to your question, it is now up to you to do the work.

   To ensure that you accomplish the task, make sure you identify a date by which you want to finish it.

   Then figure out what tasks need to be completed to crush that end goal.

   Finally, ensure that those tasks are scheduled into your day and go for it!

   STRIVE TO LEARN SOMETHING EVERY DAY!

30
ROLE MODEL

Do you consider yourself a solid role model?

Think about how your teammates view you. Do they look up to you?

Do they strive to be like you because you are an awesome leader?

THEY ARE WATCHING YOU

Being a role model is pretty cool and must be considered an honor.

We mentioned earlier that how you do anything is how you do everything.

People are watching your daily actions. Your coaches and teammates are watching your actions on the ice and in the dressing room.

When you become a role model, you are lifting up others and helping them become their best selves!

When you become extremely excited about someone else, rather than yourself, you are becoming a role model.

When you stop what you are doing and focus entirely on someone else, you are leading and others will want to speak to you.

When you are more empathetic, you will begin to feel the pain or discomfort that they are going through.

Be there for people that are hurting.

Do and say the right things!

ACTION STEPS

1) Lead by example – Through your personal actions, show everyone that only 100% effort level is tolerated.

2) Class leader - Be a leader in the classroom. Assist your teachers and help other students that are struggling.

3) Sibling power - Your little brother or sister looks up to you. Sometimes it may not seem that way because siblings don't get along all the time.

   However, stop and watch those little eyes.

   They love you and want to be like you!

   BE GREAT, SO THEY CAN BE GREAT!

31
PAST DOESN'T DEFINE YOU

Do you find yourself always thinking about the past?

When was the last time you felt bad about something that already happened?

Did you feel that an event or an outcome was affected by you and you were the reason for the failure?

The reality is that we as people, hockey players, brothers, sisters, and kids will all fail.

There will be moments that we were not proud of and wish we could have handled differently.

After the event has occurred, it should now be referred to as the PAST.

How often do you feel that the past moment defines you?

That moment has already happened and you cannot change it. If you continue to think of the past, you will create added stress and anxiety in your life.

The next question is whether anxiety is part of your life.

Anxiety can consume your thoughts, affect your ability to focus, and skew reality.

When anxiety creeps in, you may have issues breathing, tightness in your chest, and racing thoughts.

The number one thing to do is reach out and talk to someone. Do not keep these thoughts confined in your head.

Human touch and communication will help calm you down and decrease your fears.

Within this book, there are many avenues to help you unleash your potential.

You are a driven person and want to start tackling many action steps.

If you put too many tasks on your plate, you will become overwhelmed, stressed, and more likely to stop.

Identify a few items and work on them diligently, with all your focused energy, and whatever you do, know that this is not a "one person" journey.

Once you have the right people in your corner, the journey will become much more manageable.

YOUR PAST DOES NOT DEFINE YOU

Everyone on this planet has done something in the past where they did not live up to their personal standards.

That doesn't define who you are as a person. Try hard not to dwell on the past.

Stay in the moment and continue to improve each day.

ACTION STEPS

1) Anxiety Attacks –

   i) Go outside and get some fresh air.

   ii) Breathe and breathe some more. Controlled breathing can have an immediate calming effect for the body and mind.

2) Trust and talk - Do not keep these emotions to yourself. If you cannot get out of your head and continue to dwell on the past, please discuss these thoughts with someone in your life that you trust.

You do not have to overcome these emotions by yourself.

Your parents may seem hard to approach sometimes, but remember they were a kid once, just like you!

3) Focus on you! Try not to worry about what other people think. Oftentimes, we think that people are judging us for our past failures. Focus on improving your current performance; you have control over that. You cannot control what other people say, but you do control how you respond!

FOCUS ON BEING THE BEST VERSION OF YOU!

32
PERFORMANCE VS POTENTIAL

Do you feel that you have not reached your full potential?

Unfortunately, most people in life will never reach their full potential.

When we continue to do the same things each day, we limit our potential.

Let's say, you do the exact same drills, the same workout, and put in the same effort each time. Do you think you will ever reach your full potential?

Many times, people incur a form of trauma that can mold their future.

These incidents inevitably create stories that, if we are not careful, become our identity, and we believe that this is just "our reality."

Insecurities and fear become part of our persona, and this restricts us from completing the necessary tasks to reach our big goals.

Let's use a real-world hockey example.

It's late in a tournament championship game, and it has been an intense battle between the two teams. The game is tied.

You have had a tough game, and you feel that the other team took a few cheap-shots on you. You get tripped up and decide to slash the opposing player!

Off to the penalty box you go with only two minutes remaining in the game.

With only 30 seconds left in the game, the opposing team scores a "power play" goal, and your team loses.

You are devastated and many of the players are not happy with you for taking a selfish penalty at such a crucial time.

This moment is not pleasant and mentally may affect you for quite some time.

However, this "performance" certainly does not define your entire future hockey career potential.

Your takeaways should be that you need to work on emotional control.

That is what happened, you took a penalty because you did not control your emotions.

ACTION STEPS

1) It's life - Stop being so hard on yourself. Everyone makes mistakes, even your NHL role models!

   That one mistake does not define the rest of their career.

2) Strive to learn! Ask people where you can improve and be open to advice.

   Begin doing the "new things" that will move you into your "new normal"!

**CHALLENGE YOUR NORMAL AND
CREATE YOUR NEW NORMAL!**

33
HOW BAD DO YOU WANT IT?

Are you the type of person that walks the walk or talks the talk?

Do you keep saying that you are going to do this or that but never follow through?

Ask yourself, why are you not completing the things that you say you will?

Is it because they are too hard or you are scared that you may fail?

Failure is a necessary component of growth.

Your plan will not always turn out as you thought it would. There will discomfort, heartache, tears, and sore muscles.

The one mission that must not be altered is your end goal.

Do not negotiate your dreams.

When the path changes, sometimes it will not be fair.

No complaining; champions *do the work* because their dreams mean way too much to whine and complain.

No one wants to hear about it anyway.

Believe that you have *greatness* inside, and you must believe that anything is possible!

When you want something bad enough, you won't quit!

Champions like you do not quit.

That's your new recipe for success.

The word "quit" is not allowed in your vocabulary anymore.

When you remove that toxic word, your mission becomes much simpler.

When the skating drills get hard and you are sucking wind and your brain is telling you to QUIT, it is much easier to keep going because your BIG WHY is at stake if you stop too soon.

You have the advantage because the majority of players will stop when the discomfort creeps in.

Not you, you have a secret weapon, and it's just removing *one word*.

QUIT, what's that?...I don't know what that means!

ACTION STEPS

1) Remove quit! The word "quit" is now removed from your vocabulary.

2) Full effort! When times get tough in hockey, at home, or in school, you persevere or at least give your full 100% and see where the cards fall!

QUITTING IS NOT AN OPTION!

34
FAIL TO PLAN, PLAN TO FAIL

Do you have a notebook?

Go get one or ask your parents to grab one for you!

There is a saying, "if it is not recorded, it never happened."

How will you know if you are making consistent improvements if you are not measuring where you are now in relation to where you once were?

You will want to keep a simple tracking system. If you get into elaborate, full page entries, you will be less likely to continue tracking your progress.

What should I be tracking?

You can track anything that is measurable.

Here are some examples that are hockey related and other items in your life.

HOCKEY

i) Assists for the month

ii) Blocked shots per game

iii) Backchecks per game

iv) Skill sessions (i.e. stickhandle in basement)

v) Exercise sessions

vi) Have you helped other players?

vii) How often are speaking negatively to yourself?

viii) How many times did you quit?

ix) Are you continually learning?

LIFE

i) School grades

ii) Have you helped other students?

iii) Learn each day

iv) Make your bed

v) Completed your daily chores

ACTION STEPS

1) Get the notebook

2) Pick 3! Choose 3 items from the hockey and life lists and start tracking.

3) Be diligent! Be consistent and track them daily.

4) Measure it! Review your items at the end of the week. Are you happy with your progress?

   If not, make adjustments and aim to improve the next week.

5) Monthly review! Look back at the past month and assess where you did well and where you can improve.

Most People Won't Even Buy the Notebook!

START TRACKING YOUR PROGRESS AND YOU WILL DO GREAT!!

35
INTERNAL FORTITUDE

Have you ever slowed down or quit because someone else did?

Did you stop when the assigned task was completed, or did you dig a little deeper and do a few extra reps?

Did you only do what was asked of you because that is what everyone else does?

If you continue to have this mindset, you will fall in line with what is classified as "normal."

Do you think the champions just completed what was asked of them in practice and did nothing else behind the scenes?

NO CHANCE!!

You may be recognizing a pattern here.

There is something inside of you that is FREE!

It is called GRIT, and it's right there waiting for you.

No one can ever take it from you.

When you want something bad enough, you will dig deeper because there is more in the tank.

Ever heard the saying "If there is a will, there is a way"?

Do not ever give up on your dreams. They are yours, so don't let anyone tell you that you cannot achieve greatness!

There will be many hills and valleys throughout your journey.

You won't win every game but if you stay in the "game" long enough, your greatness is right around the corner!

Do what other people won't, so you can achieve what they cannot!

ACTION STEPS

1) Dream big! Write down your BIG GOAL and look at it every day!

   This is very powerful. If you write down your goal each day, you have an upwards of 40% higher chance to achieve that BIG GOAL!

2) Fail Often! There will be many moments that don't do in your favor.

   It's not failing, it is a learning opportunity.

   IF THERE IS A WILL, THERE IS A WAY!

36
HOW HARD HAVE YOU REALLY TRIED

Have you come off the ice and known that it was not your 100% effort?

Can you look in the mirror at the end of the day with a straight face, knowing you put in *your* 100% best effort in all areas of your life?

How passionate are you about improving yourself as a hockey player and as a person?

Once you become passionate about something, it is much easier to go all in!

The great thing about life is that there is always another day. Another day to wake up and make that decision to put in the work that is required to be successful.

The big kicker is that it always will come down to you!

What does 100% in hockey and life feel like?

Think back to the last time that the pucks stayed in the bag and your coach made you skate and skate some more. It felt like the drills would never end, your legs and breathing got worse and worse, but you kept grinding and grinding.

You fell to your knees, only to be told that your line is up next. You thought you couldn't do any more, but the reality is you are still alive and reading this right now.

In school, are you putting in "hockey effort"?

You may not see it or believe it, but school is so much more important than you think.

The habits we instill in our lives carry over to other areas as well.

The way you do one thing is how you do everything!

Only you know whether your 100% effort will be reached each day!

ACTION STEPS

1) Identify your PURPOSE. What is it?

   Is it to be a better team player, better scorer, on a higher-level team, or get higher school grades?

2) Look inside! When times are getting tough, you must refer to that purpose.

3) At the beginning of the day, review what your main goals are.

   At the end of the day, take a minute and review your performance.

   Did you put forth your 100%?

   PURPOSE-PASSION-EFFORT!

37
SAVE THE MONEY

How much money have you saved?

Do you have a bank account?

"Save my money... is this a financial planning book?"

Before we get to the hockey advice, yes, here is some financial advice that every kid show know.

When you receive money for your birthday, Christmas, or from your part-time job, start saving now!

Approach your parents, and ask if you can get a bank account set up.

Now, when that money comes in, take 50%, put it in the bank, and DO NOT touch it.

You can still be a kid and enjoy the other 50%. The money in the bank will keep growing, and when it's time to make a substantial purchase, you will be ahead of most of your friends.

It would be pretty cool to buy a car, wouldn't it?

Now, let's relate this to hockey.

Let's keep this super simple and to the point. What matters most is between your eyes and in your chest!

Likely you are on the ice several times per week and do not need to sign up for every single extra training session.

There are many great trainers in your local area, and you should utilize their expertise.

Choose the trainer that aligns with your goals and work with them, but not on everything because it does cost a bundle and will burn you out.

This will open up a few hours each week to focus on your current needs.

Think of this way…it will take you travel time to get to the rink, get dressed, complete the training session, undress, and drive home.

That could be two hours of your day, and of course there is a financial charge.

Have you ever heard the saying that:

"Hard work will overtake talent that does not work hard"?

What if you used that two hours in a different way that could help you move past the rest of the pack? Would you do it?

ACTION STEPS

Check out this 2-hour breakdown:

1) Read a book for 30 minutes. An example would be from Jocko Willinick, Way of the Warrior Kid.

2) Cardio training - Sprinting, biking, etc. Don't coast; push outside your comfort zone. 20 minutes.

3) Be creative! - Pick up your stick and just be a kid. Play road hockey and be creative in your basement. Have fun! 25 minutes

4) Study time - Watch videos of the greats. Start breaking down their moves, where they position themselves on the ice. Use that phone for a purpose. 25 minutes

5) Last ten minutes - Write down your goals. There have been many studies that show that if you write down your goals, you have a much higher chance of achieving them. When you see them every day, it is a constant reminder!

NOW, GO GET IT!

38
LITTLE DETAILS MATTER

When is the last time you sat down and broke down your game?

Do you even know what your strengths and weaknesses are?

It is very difficult to focus on the little things if you do not know where you are currently at.

Ok, so what are the little things anyway?

Here are several examples of the fine details that help improve many areas of your game:

i) Faceoffs

ii) Positioning in front of the net

iii) Seeing the ice better

iv) Solid backhand shot

v) Passing both forehand and backhand

vi) Honorable teammate

This activity will take some time to complete but is necessary if you want to create a tracking system for your strengths and weaknesses.

These are the "little details." Most kids your age will not be using techniques like these.

These are used by high functioning CEOs and athletes to help them achieve their personal bests year after year!

ACTION STEPS

1) Strengths and weaknesses! Write down what you think your strengths and weaknesses are. Ask your coach if they agree with your list.

2) Be specific! Choose one weakness and one strength.

    Schedule in 10 minutes each day and focus on them.

3) Be consistent! Do this for one week. If you are content with the progress, then choose a different strength and weakness to focus on.

    If not, continue to focus on the first one until it meets your standards.

    Then choose another weakness and strength and work on them each day for 10 minutes.

    Do it for a week!

4) Assessment time! After one month, reassess and write down your strengths and weaknesses.

    Again, ask the coach if they agree.

5) Make a new list and begin the above process again.

PLANING YOUR WAY TO SUCCESS!

39
YOU NEED TO SEE TO BELIEVE

Do you ever take it personally when a coach or your parent is just trying give you advice?

It happens. We don't like when people are pointing out our weak points.

Where there is weakness, there is an opportunity for strength.

Identifying your weaknesses is actually a great thing!

You need to improve to become the player that you strive to be!

If you do not believe those giving you feedback, watch it for yourself!!

Professional athletes are known to spend endless hours fine-tuning their physical fitness to ensure they can compete at the highest level. They are fast, strong, look like an athlete, and, on the exterior, look like they are ready for any battle.

What does not get mentioned is the countless hours they spend in the film room analyzing games.

Professionals do not leave the results up to chance or luck.

The greats are obsessive in learning about their opponents' strengths and weaknesses so they can exploit and use them to their advantage next time they play.

The pros also know that if they are to remain effective, they must refine their own game and improve each year. You may not have the fancy facilities of a professional team, but you do have access to devices that can record you on and off the ice.

ACTION STEPS

1) Videotape it!

    Record the game or practice.

    Now, you get to watch yourself in action.

2) Ask the tough question! If you are unable to pinpoint your strengths and weaknesses, ask a coach, parent, or friend.

    Once the strengths and weaknesses are identified, refer to Little Things Matter and follow those action steps.

    TURN THAT WEAKNESS INTO A STRENGTH!

40
DRINK THE WATER

How is your energy throughout the game and practice?

Does it feel like you just don't have the legs to finish out the game?

Do you make bad decisions and mistakes later in the game?

Well, it could be as simple as drinking more water!

Sure, it could be the fact that your cardiovascular conditioning is lacking, but not always.

If that is the case, be honest with yourself. You know if your cardio is good or not!

Let's go!

Ok, back to the water. When you get up in the morning, you have likely just slept 8-10 hours. When is the last time you were awake during the day and decided not to drink water for 10 hours?

Probably not very often, and if you do, your energy levels will be compromised.

So, when you get up in the morning, drink a big glass of water. This helps you hydrate and get rid of that groggy brain.

Make hydration a priority each day.

If your PEE is not clear, you need fluids!

This is so simple, but too often kids do not pay attention to this *little detail*.

When you are active, you will need more fluids. Keep it simple.

How do you feel?

If you feel sluggish and your pee is not clear, grab some water.

This will really make a difference on game day. Pay attention to this little detail, and you will feel better going into the game and later in the game.

ACTION STEPS

1) Re-hydrate! Drink water soon after waking up and be self-aware throughout the day.

    A simple rule of thumb is to drink 8 glasses each day, but this may vary day to day.

2) Drink it! If you are more active, drink more water.

3) Be aware! Pay attention to the color of your pee. Clear is good!

4) Buy a jug - If you have a difficult time keeping track, there are water jugs that break down the number of ounces you consumed throughout the day.

STAY HYDRATED AND STAY FRESH!

41
DARE TO COMPARE

Are you constantly comparing yourself to other people?

This is not a productive exercise because we are all different people, and you really should focus on yourself!

You don't know where they started or went through previously.

Let's, for example, look at the hockey greats that you are following.

These people should be pedestals of learning, not someone to compare yourself against!

Load up a video of your favorite player and identify one of their superior moves.

"That was a cool move, I wish I could do that." You can!

Spend the time to learn that move or technique, and then apply in it practices and games.

Boom, now you have another weapon in your arsenal.

You are running your own race, but you can certainly apply what the greats have done throughout their journeys to the top!

You only get one journey, so why would you want to feel crappy thinking about where you are in comparison to other people?

Be proud of your accomplishments!

Most people do not celebrate their wins enough!

Society tells us that we should only celebrate when we achieve something really big.

Each day you are racking up the wins!

You did some extra stickhandling, you worked on your conditioning, you watched McDavid on YouTube, you helped another player, you drank more water than usual, you made your bed, you worked your hardest in practice.

There are 7 WINS right there!!! Each day that you commit to the process, you are improving and should be *proud* of that progression.

Good for you! You may not see it, but it is happening!

ACTION STEPS

1) Record it! Write down your wins each day.

2) Assess progress! Review them at the end of the week.

3) Dare to compare! Now when you start comparing yourself, you can go back and look at all the wins that you are having day in, day out.

4) Pick a pro skill - Choose a move or skill from the pros that will heighten your game.

Practice it many times until it becomes smooth and ready to apply in your own game!

START TRACKING YOUR PROGRESS!

42
PICK THEM UP

How do you feel when you make a mistake that hurts the team?

Do you feel like you want to crawl under a rock and just hide?

It doesn't feel nice when we do something that makes us look bad!

It sucks when you feel like you have let other people down!!

So the next time someone on your team makes a mistake, remember how you felt when you made a mistake.

Be a leader and start asking, "What can I do to add value for this person?"

Adding value for others will in fact add value for you.

It may not happen right away, but this world rewards those who consistently add value in other people's lives.

At the beginning of the day, during the day, and at the end of the day, ask yourself, "How can I improve someone's life?"

It is too easy to judge and criticize other people.

It is much more effective if you place yourself in their shoes. Try to understand how you would feel if this happened to you.

The next time a teammate gives away the puck and the other team scores, do not make a negative comment. Go over to them and lift them up!

The next time the goalie lets in a weak goal, go smack them on the pads and say "It's ok, let's get the next one, we need you!"

Negative energy will go through your team quickly... but so does POSTIVE ENERGY!

ACTION STEPS

1) Raise them up! Lift up people when they are in despair.

2) Who are you? Are you a negative energy player or do you lift up the team?

   ASK YOURSELF - "Who can I help today?"

3) Not just hockey - Helping should be in all areas of your life.

   It applies in the classroom, at school, and definitely at home with your family.

NEGATIVE WORDS CAN AFFECT PEOPLE FOR MUCH LONGER THAN JUST THAT MOMENT

43
BUILD THE TEAM

Are you aware of your role on the team?

Do you feel left out or confused regarding what the coach is asking you to do?

If that is the case, raise your hand and ask the coach!

If you are uncomfortable with that approach, schedule a private meeting with the coach. It is very important that you understand the expectations of the coaching staff.

When each person understands their job role within the team, there is a much greater chance that your team will be successful.

It is very uncommon that championships will be won without great team chemistry and everyone doing *their* job!

This also makes it much simpler for each teammate to perform at their highest level. Once you are dialed in on your job, you are not trying too hard to complete other roles that are not your responsibility.

Focus on doing *your* job very well and let your teammates excel at theirs.

If you are not a goal scorer, then don't worry about being a goal scorer.

Stay focused on your tasks. If you do your tasks very well, you will still have opportunities to score!

Be the best teammate you can be. If all players have this mentality, your team will begin to operate as a well-oiled machine.

ACTION STEPS

1) Do you know! If you do not know your job role on the team, you must ask the coach.

2) Study time - Once you are clear on your job role, start researching the "greats" that had the same responsibilities as you.

   Learn from the best. Watch YouTube, read articles and books, and then focus on the information that you attained.

3) Team building! Do your job really well so the team has a better chance of succeeding.

   If everyone is a team player and does their job well, individual opportunities open up for everybody.

GO ALL IN FOR THE TEAM!

44
TRUTH MAY HURT

What is one area of your game that needs work?

Oftentimes, it is difficult to analyze our own game and determine where we need the most work.

Have you ever been driving home and your parents are on your case regarding your performance?

This can be annoying can't it!

But, they are watching you play day in and day out and they may be seeing things that you are not. They are just trying to help, so you can become a more well-rounded player.

If you don't want to hear it from your parents, reach out to your coach or another teammate.

The advice you receive may hurt and difficult to accept.

However, if want to continue to improve, you must become aware of the areas that need work.

Instead of taking it personally, become a curious student. Every player has weaknesses on and off the ice. When people take time to try to improve your game, remain humble and listen.

When you become open-minded to the possibilities of improvement, your path to success becomes wider and easier to travel down.

It may be difficult to keep your mouth shut and hear about your deficiencies. If you argue and defend yourself, the person giving the feedback will often retract and your learning lesson is over!

The best learners seek feedback and listen intently because they are on a mission.

They want to learn daily, weekly, and make sure they have improved every month.

This approach will lead to many more growth opportunities.

The first step is to ASK, next up is LISTEN, and finally DO THE WORK!

ACTION STEPS

1) Raise that hand! Ask your parents, coaches, and teammates where you can improve.

2) It is not personal! The feedback is not a personal attack.

    It is much easier to build a self-improvement plan if you know where you are failing.

LOOK INSIDE, THAT IS WHERE THE GROWTH STARTS!

45
STUDY AND STUDY SOME MORE

Have you been working extremely hard but are frustrated with the results?

Do you feel you should be further ahead by now?

You may just be overlooking one skill that could catapult you to the next level!!

Who are the best players in the NHL? Who are the best players in your city?

NHL players have played much longer than you and have had access to very high-level coaching. They have worked on their skills thousands of times.

They have completed the repetitions and now have refined them.

Once they refine the skills, they don't continue doing it the wrong way.

So, you have the opportunity to learn from the best players in the game and start emulating their tried and true, tested skills.

Your efforts may not be pretty the first time or maybe even the tenth, but if you stick with it, your skillset will vastly improve when you have the top mentors!

Use your phone as a hockey education tool. It's not just about who you decide to follow, it's what they have to offer.

Once you identify the areas that you need to improve in, research players that are strong in that specific area.

Pick a skill and break down the skill into steps. The technique or skill you are trying to emulate has many components built into it. Refine Step #1, #2, #3, and so on.

Once you have refined this new skill, start applying it into your own practices and games.

Often, players become complacent and only use their team practices as their learning ground.

Maintaining a thirst for information and advancement will separate the great players from the good ones!

ACTION STEPS

1) Learn from them! What part of your games needs assistance?

2) Open your eyes! Watch the greats on video and write down the areas that they excel at.

3) One to begin! Choose one of those skills to focus on, and don't be tempted to choose more.

4) Do the work! Start working on refining that skill in your game every day.

   Schedule it in!

5) Apply it - You have done the work, so now it's time to use these skills in a game situation.

   Play Like A PRO!

6) Improvements! Once you are happy with the progress, choose another skill to improve.

LEARN FROM THE BEST TO BE THE BEST!

46
TREAT IT LIKE SCHOOL

Nooooo, not school!

When you look at your school schedule, there are specific classes at certain hours each day. It is set up this way to ensure that the class takes place and students show up on time.

Attending class on a consistent basis gives each student the opportunity to learn.

Now, not a lot of players in your league will utilize this approach for hockey development. You will have a distinct advantage if you start scheduling in personal growth sessions!

If you do not plan it and schedule it in, most times it will never happen.

Here is an example in relation to passing:

ACTION STEPS

1) YouTube wisely! Research passing drills. Make sure you choose a reputable respected resource.

2) Buy the notebook! Write down the areas within that skill that you can improve.

   i) Forehand pass

   ii) Backhand pass

   iii) Sauce pass

    iv) Drop pass

    v) Backdoor pass

    vi) Behind the net passes

3) Short times! Schedule in just 10 minutes each day to work on passing.

If you look at your day, there are definitely 10 minutes available, probably much more.

If you want to increase your focus time to 15-20 minutes, make sure you take a 5-minute break before the next session.

How much time are you on your phone each day doing mindless activities?

Before you know it, there will have been five or six 10-minute sessions completed. That is only one hour of your entire day, leaving much time to spend with friends and focusing on other aspects of life that you love!

A little planning will catapult you past those who wake up each day with no plan.

If you want to be great, use your time wisely.

USE THIS ADVANTAGE AND MOVE FORWARD QUICKLY!

47
THE PHONE IS A TOOL

Ok, let's get this out in the open!!

How much time do you spend on your phone each day?

If you do not know the exact time, track it for a whole week and determine your daily average. You may be quite surprised!

No, I am not trying to act like your parent. (Well, I kinda am ☺)

I am trying to show you how much time you are wasting each day.

Identifying where you spend your time becomes an *advantage* you will have over the competition!

For example, if your current screen time is 2.5 hours and your competition's is 2.5 hours, you are both on the same playing field, right?

For now, until you take the action steps below!

Ok, you still need to be a kid and enjoy time with your friends and playing a few games online.

So, here is how you level up and pass your competition.

ACTION STEPS

1) Pay attention! Track your screen time for a week to acquire your daily average.

2) Start slow! If it was 2.5 hours, reduce it to 1.5 hours.

3) Schedule it! Then use that extra 1 hour each day to improve

your game. It could be stickhandling, cardio work, researching the greats, shooting or passing.

If you do this, you will have 7 extra hours per week of focused work on your game.

That's 28 hours per month and a grand total of 362 hours for the YEAR!!

PUT THE PHONE DOWN AND CONQUER THE COMPETITION!

48
HOLD YOURSELF ACCOUNTABLE

What is one skill that you really want to improve this month?

Ok, now that you have identified the task, you must hold yourself accountable to do what you said you are going to do!

This may be a lot easier than you think.

First, you must tell someone what your plan is.

Someone who is important to you and you do not want to let down.

This could be your parents, your coach, a friend, or possibly a sibling.

When we tell people our plan, they can hold us accountable, plus no one enjoys letting people down and looking silly.

Make sure that your GOAL is set just outside your comfort zone. Something that is attainable if you work your tail off.

Write this GOAL down so you see it every day. It needs to be written down somewhere that is visible and in plain sight.

The probability of achievement substantially increases if you simply write it down daily!

Not just a little, a lot! There have been many studies completed, and those who write down their GOALS daily or at least have them in plain sight (like on a calendar) will in fact have an upwards of 40% higher probability of fulfilling that dream!

ACTION STEPS

1) Post the GOAL! It could be on the wall where you hang your equipment to dry.

2) Post it in the area where you frequently practice at home.

3) Post it in your closet where you get dressed (if you do not want others to see it).

4) Record daily! Write it down in a notebook each day.

5) Mirror each day - At the end of the day, look at yourself in the mirror.

Did you put forth your 100% effort today?

100% EFFORT, ONLY YOU KNOW!

49
ACCOUNTABILITY COACH

Have you ever had someone hold you accountable to what you said you were going to do?

Do you have a goal in mind but month after month you do not achieve what you are hoping?

This is very normal, so do not feel bad.

Did you catch the word that was used there? "Normal."

You are reading this book because you do not want to be viewed as a "normal" hockey player, is that right!!

If you want to stay normal and keep floating through year after year with no progress, go right ahead. Most people in society live their whole lives this way, and no one really criticizes them because they can still do well being "normal."

However, if you want to achieve exceptional results in the hockey world, you shouldn't have to do it on your own. ASK for help!

Why not have someone else in your corner, rooting for you and keeping you accountable to the dreams that you deserve!

Who should that person be? Well, that's up to you. It could be your parents, a coach, a friend, or a teammate.

The key is picking someone who will not let you slide and slither out of what you said you would do.

It is advantageous to choose someone who holds themselves accountable too. They are viewed as unstoppable in all areas in your life.

Seek out this high-performer and get them into your corner!

Make sure they have no problem calling you out on your INACTIONS!

ACTION STEPS

1) Be honest! Identify the skills you want to improve upon.

2) Choose wisely! Pick an accountability coach.

3) Open up! Tell them the areas that you want them to hold you accountable on.

4) Consistency is key! Check in with them weekly.

5) Build a team! Do not let them down, because if you do, you are also letting yourself down.

CONSISTENT ACTION LEADS TO CONSISTENT IMPROVEMENT

50
GET SOME SLEEP

Do you know other kids that are staying up super late and think it's so cool?

"But, so-and-so goes to bed at 1 AM, and he is doing fine!"

He may be doing well right now, but this approach will catch up with them in the long term, and their performance level will be affected.

Research has proven that any sleep that you can get before midnight is much more valuable than the hours after midnight.

What time are you currently going to bed?

How do you feel when you get up, are you energized and ready to go?

You may think this is just a parental tactic to get you to go to bed!!

You are an athlete, working hard and pushing yourself each day.

If you expect your body to perform at a high level, you need to treat it with respect.

Eating healthy foods and providing your body with adequate rest and recovery is often overlooked.

So, start paying attention to your body. How do you feel when you get up?

How do you feel in the afternoon, are you starting to crash?

Finally, how do you feel going to the rink before the big game?

Are you ready to go or do you feel sluggish?

Take care of your body, and the results will take care of themselves!!

Who cares if someone else is up until midnight playing around on their phone…you will fly by these people!!

ACTION STEPS

1) Just go! Aim to go to bed at the same time each night and get up at the same time each morning.

2) Make it a habit! Aim to get more than 8 hours of sleep each night.

3) You won't miss much! If you are tired, go to bed. If you want to be a high-performance athlete, you will need to make a few sacrifices.

4) Have a nap! If you are getting up early and working out hard, there will be times when you are tired. Many high-level athletes and CEOs awake early and work very hard and have used napping as another high-level tool.

You only need a ten to fifteen-minute session. You will be surprised at the energy spike afterwards.

Listen to your body! You may benefit from one to two short naps each day!

YOU CAN'T KEEP YOUR EYES OPEN, GO TO BED!

51
VALUE YOUR SUCCESS

What are you currently doing after success has been achieved?

Are you content with that level and start to take it easy and relax?

You deserve that rest, don't you? "All my hard work, sweat, and sore muscles! I need a rest, and I am entitled to it!"

To a point, this is true…stay with me here.

You set a goal and did the necessary work, day in and day out, to achieve the level you were aiming for. This meant that you had to push yourself outside your comfort zone. You completed the extra sessions in the basement and driveway, especially when no one was watching. You followed a healthy eating lifestyle and went to bed when most others were playing on their phones.

You had a plan and stuck to it, and look at you now, you made it!

That is awesome that you stuck with it, most people do not and quit way too early!

When you are successful, you have to remember all the systems that were in place to help move you up to that level. If you think that you will just be successful from now on, you have another thing coming.

Do not forget or get rid of the things that you completed on the road to your success.

For example, let's say that you identified stickhandling and edgework as your weaknesses.

You put a plan in place and stuck with it. You got up 20 minutes early and practiced stickhandling before going to school every day!

You enrolled in a power skating program and improved your edgework.

People noticed and you are now on the first line. Sure, your hard work paid off and you are reaping the rewards, but it's not over.

You still have not reached your personal potential.

Keep going!! Identify the next area that needs improvement and use the same approach you did to accomplish the first one!

Challenge yourself! You have a lot more in the tank!

ACTION STEPS

1) Enjoy it! Once you reach your goal (success), celebrate it, you do deserve it!

   If you celebrate too long, you will start taking for granted what got you there in the first place!

2) Don't forget! Always remember the steps that you took along the way to that successful moment.

3) Study them! Research the habits of successful hockey players.

   The great ones continue striving to become better and better.

**CELEBRATE YOUR SUCCESSES,
THEN GET BACK TO BUSINESS!**

52
QUALITY VS QUANTITY

When you go to a skill-building session or extra skate, are you just a number?

What I mean by that is, what is the coach/player ratio?

These sessions are expensive. and you deserve great service!

When the ratio becomes too high, the attention to detail for each player is lost.

You are going through the motions of the drills but not receiving much feedback on your performance.

If this is the case, don't be afraid to ask that coach if they can make sure you are doing the drills correctly.

At the end of the day, you are in their program because you want to improve and deserve to know if you are getting better.

Ideally, when signing up for development sessions, the coach/player ratio should be on the lower end.

One-on-one sessions can get pricey, so team up with a few buddies to reduce the cost. When there are fewer players, the coach can really dive deep into the individual's current level to put a plan in place to help you reach your desired outcome!

Finally, when you are involved in development sessions, treat them like a competition!

Why are you doing these sessions anyway?

Likely, it is to become a better player and excel, which means surpassing your competition.

When you attend these sessions, always strive to be the hardest worker and soak up all the knowledge that is being offered!

You have hired a coach who has a higher-level knowledge base, that is why they are now instructing.

Ask them what it takes to be great. Ask them what you need to work on at home.

Ask them about their own hockey path. Ask them what served them well and what did not. Ask them if they could change one thing, what would it be?

To achieve greatness, always remain a student!

ACTION STEPS

1) It's about you! Choose the right program for you. Don't just do it because other people are.

2) You deserve the attention! Evaluate the coach/player ratio.

3) Competition time - Be the hardest worker in the program.

You are there to learn and become a better version of yourself.

HARDEST WORKER IN THE ROOM, LET'S GO!

53
WHO IS WATCHING

Has a coach or parent ever said to you, "Play hard, you never know who is watching"?

This statement holds a lot of truth to it because you never know who is in the stands.

When you are on a team, that does not guarantee that you will be on that team forever.

Other players develop, coaching staff changes, so what is currently happening right now may not be reality the next year.

There may be someone in the stands who has applied to be the coach for your age group the following year.

They may have seen you stop two feet short on the forecheck. They saw you coast on the backcheck. They know it wasn't the goalie's fault; you could have caught them at the blueline.

Now, be careful using this strategy as your main strategy to excel on the ice.

Sure, there may be someone up in the stands looking down critiquing all the players; you can't control who watches your games.

What you can control is your effort.

A longer-term approach is that your effort is never compromised.

If you are putting forth your best game, it doesn't matter who is watching.

You know that you couldn't have done anything else!

The only person that can protect your dreams is you!

When put your head on the pillow each night, you should be able to smile knowing that personally you gave 100% in all areas of your life!

If you are not at ease with your current effort levels, you may need to assess what is really important to you.

What are you truly passionate about and enjoy doing?

If you cannot get excited about it, that path may not be for you.

ACTION STEPS

1) No shift off! Do not take a game off. You won't always have a great game, but you do have control over your effort level.

2) Nothing is for sure! Do not expect that you will be on the same team every year.

   Nothing is guaranteed!

3) You have control! Protect those big goals by putting forth your full effort in all aspects of life.

   Be honest, only you know what your 100% looks like.

   IT BEGINS WITH YOUR EFFORT, THEY WILL NOTICE!

54
FLY, SWIM, GROW

What are you talking about, fish and birds?

When is the last time you went to the grocery store with your parents?

Have you paid attention to how the aisles are set up?

Next time they go shopping, go with them.

You will soon notice that the healthy non-processed foods are around the outside aisles. The processed garbage is located on the inner aisles with strategic items placed at the end of the aisles. Don't let them get you!

A good rule of thumb is to ask yourself, "Does it fly, swim, or grow?"

These are items that our bodies will recognize. Our bodies will be able to process these foods much easier and break them down for useable energy.

Go pick up a package in the inner aisle and read the ingredients.

Half the time, you will not even be able to pronounce the words, so how do you expect your body to accept and use that food?

If your parents continue to buy packaged garbage food, set aside a time to talk to them. Explain to them that you want to perform at a higher level and would like them to make an effort to buy natural, healthy foods.

The whole family will be better off for it!

This is simply a guideline, and it may be beneficial to hire a nutritionist who can assist in setting up a healthy eating plan for you and your family.

Your body will recover more easily.

You will have more energy and your performance will greatly improve.

Preparation is critical.

What should I be eating?

When should I be eating it?

Is the healthy food available to me?

ACTION STEPS

1) Take a trip! Go to the grocery store and take a look at what is in the outer aisles.

   Then go take a look at all the man-made garbage in the inner store.

2) Living organism! If it flies, swims, or grows, add it to your healthy eating lifestyle.

3) Healthy habits! You are choosing a healthy lifestyle, not a diet!

EAT TO PERFORM!

55
HABIT OVERHAUL

Are you aware of your poor daily habits?

Are you aware of the good habits that are part of your lifestyle?

How are you supposed to know what a poor habit looks like compared to a solid habit?

They have been mentioned many times already, but let's recap to ensure you are not wasting time each day!

The biggest challenge for you will be your phone.

When you use it for its true intention, you have such a valuable tool right at your fingertips.

If you start using it for mindless activities, you are wasting time.

It is ok to have fun, and you should, life is short.

However, you have made the decision to become the best person and player possible.

You will need to resist temptation. Remember, if the average kid is spending 2.5 hours per day on screen and you cut your hours back to 1.5, you have a huge advantage.

You will have 362 hours extra per year! That is a huge advantage over the competition.

We will get into more habits in another chapter, but for now, get a handle on the screen time!

Your phone is a distraction but only one habit that needs to be assessed.

Each person in this world has 24 hours per day, just like you.

Successful people use their time wisely. They may not be any smarter or talented than the next person, but they utilize the precious minutes within their day.

Let's do a simple daily breakdown of an efficient day for a kid!

But first, to fully understand your current efficiency level, you must track your daily activities and write down the time that was spent on that activity.

The biggest time suckers will be phone screen time and TV.

Carry around a little notebook and track your whole day and do this for both a school weekday and for the weekend.

Be honest because your dreams depend on it!

ACTION STEPS

1) Limit screen time. Identify your current daily screen time. Cut it in half!

2) Grow each day! Spend the extra hour on personal development.

   Break down the hour and assign time blocks for specific skills.

3) Don't be tempted!! When you are training and refining skills, put your phone in another room.

   Do not become distracted, you have a job to do. Let's go!

DAILY PLANNING EXAMPLE (These times won't be exact for you, but the structure should look similar)

   7:00am- Wake up

   7:00-7:15- Hydrate with two glasses of water

   7:15-7:45- Work on an area that needs improvement

7:45- Shower

8:00- Healthy breakfast and surf phone before school

9:00-3:30- School focus

3:45-4:30- Homework

4:30-5:00- Use completed homework as a reward to now focus on a passion. This could be a hockey skill or another area that you passionate about.

5:00-5:30- Dinner time with family

5:30- Help clean kitchen

6:00-7:00- Finish homework

7:00-7:30- Physical fitness

7:30- Fun time (phone, friends, etc.)

9:00 or so- Lights out

Lots of time for self-improvement in the classroom, hockey, and physical fitness, and look, there was still lots of time to be a kid!

THE PHONE IS A TOOL, NOT AN ADDICTION!

56
BE A DREAMER

How often do you find yourself daydreaming?

Many people feel that this is a waste of time, but if done correctly, it will be a valuable tool for you.

First, ask yourself what you are dreaming about.

If it is eating a pizza or something like that, yes, that is not very productive.

Now, close your eyes and think of the big hockey goals you have, the big life goals you have…

These goals are essentially your dreams. It is ok to dream big, because who wants to be normal anyway!!

Here is the big takeaway: write them down, now!

Most people have dreams and goals, but they never happen.

They just stay in your head, floating around. When you write them down, they become real.

Write your dream on paper and post it in a place where you will see it each day.

To make it even more powerful, attach a DUE DATE.

Set the date to when you want to achieve this dream.

If you do not meet the exact date, that is ok because at least you are making progress towards your dream.

Dream big, put a plan in place, and work hard each day!

Make the simple promise to NEVER QUIT!

Difficult situations will arise and not everyone will believe in you or your dreams.

Do you believe that you have what it takes?

Keep dreaming because daydreaming is free. Dream big and visualize yourself already achieving your biggest goals.

ACTION STEPS

1) Dreams are great! Let your mind wander; this is natural.

2) Dream big! Identify your major dreams and write them out. Post it in sight.

3) Review often! The brain is a very powerful tool if used wisely.

Start envisioning yourself already achieving that dream.

If you think it, believe it, and do the work, it will become reality.

BE A DREAMER, THEN DO IT!

57
BE THE DIFFERENCE MAKER

How does it feel when your actions were the difference in the game?

Wouldn't it be amazing if you could feel this way more often?

It feels great knowing that your efforts are making a difference.

We like to be noticed, recognized, and deemed the MVP, or should I say the MVT (we will get to that in a moment.)

To be a difference maker, you need to be very aware of what is going on around you.

If you are super aware, you begin to recognize what is needed to make the difference!

Here are a few examples:

1) There are patterns of negative energy on and off the ice.

    You have the opportunity to flip the negative into positive energy. Positivity turns into smiles and players having more fun.

    Hockey players who have more fun will have more energy and their performance will be lifted.

2) The other team is getting too many shots. Ask yourself, "What can I do to help limit the amount of shots on our net?"

    Personally, I can go out and block a few shots, dominate the backcheck, and cover the player I am responsible for.

    Also, speak up and let your team know that you all need to limit these shots.

Then go out and lead by example!

3) Let's stay on the idea of leading by example because this is the most important.

If you strive to be the hardest worker in practice and games, other players notice.

They constantly see that you will never quit, and they too will begin to play like this.

Hard work and positivity breed hard work and positivity!

You become the difference maker solely because of your work ethic!

The difference maker on the team is not the MVP, they are the MVT: the Most Valuable Teammate!

ACTION STEPS

1) Look around! Start paying attention in the dressing room and on the ice.

   Start asking yourself, "How can I be the difference maker?"

2) ASK - If you want more feedback on what it takes to be an awesome teammate, ask your coach, ask other teammates, or I bet Google will have many answers too:

   Here are a few to consider:

   i) Lead by example

   ii) Understand and do your role well

   iii) Be positive

   iv) Be prepared

   v) Hardest worker in the room

   vi) Be accountable for your actions

vii) Hold others accountable

3) Team effort! Do it for the team!

Playing for yourself is selfish and not positive for your development or your team!

4) Little details! Block the shot, take the extra step, be positive, and lead by example.

LEAD FROM THE FRONT!

58
PROVE YOURSELF

Have you ever felt like other people do not believe in you?

Do they feel that you do not deserve where you are at?

This can be hurtful and often you may start second-guessing yourself on and off the ice.

Unfortunately, you cannot control how other people speak about you or even to you.

But the great thing is that you have full control over how you will respond to them or, better yet, how you do not respond to them at all.

Who are they to judge you and say harsh things about you?

In a perfect world, all people would be positive, uplifting, and supportive of your dreams.

Sorry, there will always be negative people. Maybe they don't want you to succeed, but more likely they are upset because they have not reached their full potential, and they are using harsh words to bring other people down.

Avoid the NAYSAYERS!!

Start hanging around people that do what you to succeed, people that have big dreams, just like you!

You don't need to prove anything to the naysayers.

Prove yourself to yourself!

If you have a dream, do not give up on it because someone else says that you cannot do it.

You decide how much effort you will put in each day. If you are consistent and give 100% effort and attention to your dream, it will become reality.

Most people give up on their dreams too early!

Comparing yourself to other people is also dangerous. You don't know where they started or what they have been through.

Don't compare, instead, only look left and right to acquire the necessary help!

Do you want to become a more prolific goal scorer or playmaker?

Reach out to the snipers and set up specialists and pick their brains.

Do you love a certain subject in school and want to become even better in that area? Reach out to those that are specialists in that subject and again pick their brains and learn as much as possible.

Then, reach out to another guru in that subject matter and learn even more and more!

This applies in school, hockey, and whatever career path you choose!

You will become the product of the five closest people you hang out with!!

ACTION STEPS

1) Who is negative? Identify the negative people in your life.
   Limit the amount of time spent with them.

2) Thick skin! Don't take it personally!

   People say mean things for many reasons, and you cannot control that.

   You do, however, control how you respond.

   The more that you show them that they cannot get underneath

your skin, the more that their power is slowly being taken away.

3) Find them! For whichever area in life that you want to improve, there are many experts available from whom you can acquire the proper advice.

Choose wisely and sit back and listen...then apply the information and never stop learning!

AVOID THE NAYSAYERS!

59
HAVE FUN

Are stilling having lots of fun playing hockey?

Is it as much fun as it was when you were a little kid?

Let's hope so, because this is the reason we signed up in the first place!

Unfortunately, it happens along the way, but you don't have to feel like this forever.

Remember when you loved going to the arena? Hopefully you still feel this way.

Think back to when you were younger and you couldn't wait to get dressed and start flying around the ice. You had a smile on your face and were having the time of your life.

If you are feeling down right now, it is important to figure out why.

Is it because someone else got to play the last shift of the game?

Did you miss a shot that could have won the game?

Are other people better than you?

Really, this list could be endless.

The important part is that you figure out WHY you are not as happy as you used to be.

Many people in this world will never step on the ice. They may not even have an arena to play in.

Start, by cherishing the fact that you do get to lace up your skates and play this awesome game!

In the whole scheme of life, the most important part of hockey is having fun!

Why would you continuing doing anything in life that makes you miserable?

Finally, when you are having fun playing sports, your performance is better.

There are chemicals in our bodies that are released when we are positive, smiley people!

When you are in the position to truly love everything about the game, you are in a position for unknown, unrecognizable growth.

Have FUN and LOVE IT! Love everything about it!

Love the challenge, love the grind, love the sweat, love the success, love the failure because that is opportunity to learn, love the feeling from a blocked shot, love the lactic acid in those legs, love the heartbreak, love the team, love the joy of a game winner, love the devastation because you know there will be another time, love the unknown, love the uncertainty, love the GAME!!

Most importantly, love the moment and the process!

ACTION STEPS

1) Good times! Close your eyes and remember the times when you were little, smiling ear to ear skating down the ice.

    When you are feeling down and things are not going your way, think of those times.

    Stop taking everything so seriously. Hockey should be fun.

2) Looks good on you! Smile for 30 seconds. You will feel better and in a more positive state.

3) Speak up! Say it out loud. If you want to feel a certain way, just say it.

Try saying it 5-10 times, and you will feel better.

"I feel great!"

Avoid the negative things you say to yourself. The brain is a powerful tool, and you will start feeling that way!

FEEL GOOD, LOOK GOOD, PLAY GOOD!

60
DO IT RIGHT THE FIRST TIME

When you are asked to do something, do you complete it with 100% effort or do you just finish because you were asked to?

Do you make your bed each day and help around the house?

You may be asking, how is making my bed or sweeping the floor going to make me a better hockey player?

When you complete tasks with your best effort, you begin taking pride in everything you do.

When you wipe a counter, you move the cup and make sure the whole counter is clean.

When you make your bed, you take ownership and make sure the corners are neat and you could bounce a quarter off it!

When you begin doing things right the first time, you begin setting a higher standard for yourself.

If you take pride and ownership in everyday tasks, this attention to detail will also happen when you are developing your hockey game.

There won't be any cutting corners, because CHAMPIONS don't stop two feet short of the line during practice.

Champions don't learn only half a skill and say, "That's good enough."

Champions do not give up because they are tired. If you want to be a champion, you will have to perform late in the third period when you are tired.

Giving up in practice is not an option. When you give up in practice, you will be more likely to give up in the game.

You may have heard the saying "practice makes perfect."

"Practice makes permanent" is more fitting.

Everything you do behind the scenes in your life will become second nature in the heat of the battle!

ACTION STEPS

1) Up to you! Make a conscious effort to put your best into everyday tasks.

2) Don't cheat! Do not cut corners in practice or when you are working on skills in the driveway or basement.

3) ASK - This again is suggested because you truly may not know if you are cutting corners.

   Ask your parents, ask your coach, ask your teacher, ask a sibling, ask a friend, ask a mentor!!

PERMANANT CHANGE!

61
GRIT IS FREE

What does it mean when someone says, "They have heart"?

Do you feel that you have heart and always grind it out, no matter what?

Is heart something that can be taught or is it something that you have at the beginning?

Do you want to know what coaches value the most in a player?

It is GRIT and yes, if you do not have it now, you can still get it!

Grit is when you keep grinding, no matter what.

Your team could be up by 2 or down by 2, you grind it out every shift because that is who you are. You are a grinder, not a floater!

The cool thing about GRIT is that it is free.

It is up to you and you only to decide if you will grind when you are tired, when your legs are jelly, and when your team needs it the most!

But, what if GRIT is not part of your current game?

Here are your action steps to become the gritty, relentless beast that you want to be:

ACTION STEPS

1) YOUR PURPOSE! If you have not identified your purpose...do it now!

   If your purpose is very strong, it is much easier to dig deep when times get tough.

2) Name of the game! Play for the name on the front and back of your jersey.

   What's your name? From now on, when people say it, they will automatically envision you being the hardest worker. Let's GO!

   When times get tough, play for the name on the front of the jersey.

   When you go all in for your teammates, the GRIT becomes contagious throughout your team!

3) Stop complacency - Never stop striving to become a better player, a better student, a better friend, a better kid, which all add up to a better person!

BE PURPOSEFUL!

62
CHANGE YOUR MIND

What will happen if you always stay the same?

What happens if you do the same thing over and over?

Honestly, not much!

If you want to improve, you must do things that you normally do not do.

If you continue doing the minimum, you will not get much better and certainly not reach your full potential. You deserve to become the best version of yourself!

When you are living comfortably and enjoying success, it is difficult to step back and say "What else can I do to improve?"

A simple way to actively improve is to actively learn.

Making this simple commitment will keep you on the path to self-improvement.

Every day, you must view situations as learning experiences, especially the tough situations.

If you want to be a champion, start thinking like a champion.

Champions raise their hands and ask the difficult but much needed questions.

When is the last time you truly asked people something because you wanted to learn, not because you had to?

Do not get too comfortable in your current situation. There are so many people out there that have knowledge in the exact areas where you are trying to improve.

Seek out those people and pick their brains.

It may be your coach, another player from an older age group, or your parents.

What are the CONSEQUENCES if you decide to just stay in your comfort bubble and be content with normal?

You will NOT reach your full potential or the heights that you are dreaming to reach which certainly will affect your daily happiness!

You must also become obsessive about your dream.

In life, there will be people that go above and beyond the normal and they will inevitably accomplish many feats that once seemed unreachable.

MENTOR TIP

When you acquire a mentor, you have access to someone who is or was great in that area of expertise.

When you are working away on a hockey skill, a drill in practice, helping a teammate, battling in the corner, or skating late in a game, you must ask yourself, what would my mentor do?

How hard would they be working? Would they be going above and beyond?

Finally, ask yourself, "Would my mentor be proud of me?"

"Would they approve of the effort that I just put in?"

ACTION STEPS

1) Raise your hand daily! Strive to learn something new each day.
   This is not just for hockey.
   Raise your hand in the classroom and at home!

2) Learn daily! At the end of the day, write down what you learned today.

   If you write it down, there is a record of your progression.

3) Do the work! After you learn something, it is up to YOU to get the wheels in motion.

4) Mentor - Would they be proud of or disappointed in your effort?

ASK THE QUESTION AND DO THE WORK!

63
BENCH YOUR EGO

How often are you checking your stats?

Do you feel that if your name is on the scoresheet that means you had a good game?

Success and personal growth are not measured by statistics and numbers.

It doesn't matter what you look like as a player on "paper."

Are your actions making an impact and making your team better.

Just because you scored a goal, that doesn't mean that your team is improving.

What matters the most is what is inside of you. Grit and determination are inside all of us, ready to be tapped into.

Your "never give up" work ethic will have a direct impact on all the players around you.

When you realize that everyone is in this together, everything becomes much simpler.

All players have important roles and if they do them very well, the team will be successful.

It doesn't matter who puts the puck in the net.

Playing with honor, integrity and a burning desire to grow will serve you well on the ice and off the ice.

Have you ever seen a player racing over to the referee to make sure that they recorded their number on the scoresheet.

That is self-serving and not an honorable attribute for a teammate.

It's about building "team spirit", not about the scoreboard.

Grit and determination are always free.

When they become part of your arsenal, you will excel and others will take notice.

Grit and Determination Are Also Contagious!

ACTION STEPS

1) Less Thinking, More Doing! Stop focusing the things that you can't do, go all in on what you can do and do them to the best of your ability.

2) Maybe Means Yes! Do not ever give up on a play, in practice and in all games.

   There is always a chance and when you always go 100%, the breaks will start to go your way.

   The other team will also notice that your team will never quit and this can take the wind out of their sails.

3) Are You Making a Difference? Is your current effort level making a difference?

   Are you improving? Is the team improving?

   What areas can you make more of an impact.

64
ACCEPT YOURSELF

How often do you compare yourself to other people?

Do you feel like you are not as good as other people?

How does this make you feel?

Stop and really think about it...

If other people's success and current status does not affect how you feel, that is fantastic. You are focusing on yourself and accepting who you are.

Try not to worry about what other people are doing and where they are at right now in their lives. We all have stories. Focus on your story, and you will become more carefree.

Do you ever have that feeling in your chest that affects your breathing?

That is stress and anxiety, and you do not deserve to live in that state.

STOP COMPARING AND REDUCE YOUR STRESS!

Also, if you feel stress and anxiety coming on, get outside and get some fresh air.

Do some controlled breathing exercises. Even if you do not have anxiety, a few minutes of deep breathing will help you become more peaceful and patient.

If you constantly compare yourself to other people, you will limit your happiness. We all have strengths and weaknesses, and people are not always at the same stage.

Focus on your current stage!

This is easier said than done, isn't it?

Don't worry, changing this mindset will not happen overnight.

Start being more aware of when you are comparing and judging other people.

Think how you feel when people do this to you.

Remember what your Mom has told you: "Treat people like you want to be treated."

Other people are more like you than you may believe. They, too, have something going on inside, just like you.

Accepting yourself, your strengths, and weaknesses will help you live in a more peaceful state.

ACTION STEPS

1) Who are you? Write down your strengths and weaknesses.

    Yes, you will have weaknesses; we all do.

    Accept who you are!

2) Don't judge!

    Other people have weaknesses just like you.

    Build them up, don't break them down!

3) Laugh at yourself!

    When you fully accept your silly attributes, you are on the way to more happiness!

4) Just breathe - Anxiety and stress are a part of life and can be overwhelming.

    i) Tell someone about it

ii) Get outside into fresh air

iii) Incorporate deep breathing into daily routine

DON'T WORRY, BE HAPPY!

65
BE REPSECTFUL

How do you treat other people?

Are you treating them as you would like to be treated?

If everyone were kind and treated people with respect, we would be living in very harmonious world, wouldn't we?

We know this is not true, and some people are just not very nice.

You have the choice to treat people in a way that is respectful and kind.

You cannot control other people's actions, but you always have the choice to control your own!

When we place our belief in other people and lovingly want them to succeed, we build deeper and more meaningful relationships.

Lift people up, remain enthusiastic and supportive of their dreams.

You must reach out to people for assistance to accomplish your dreams, so be there wholeheartedly when someone needs your help!

Here are a few real-life examples of things that you can do daily:

ACTION STEPS

1) Look up! Look people in the eye when they are speaking to you.

2) Respect! When you meet someone, shake their hand firmly and look them in the eye.

3) Be kind! Open the door and hold it for people.

4) Superiors! When you address an adult, call them "Mr." or "Mrs." until told otherwise.

5) Help! If someone needs help, take time to help them out. They have dreams to!

JUST BE NICE!

66
THE BULLY

Have you ever encountered the team bully?

Are you the team bully?

Bullying frequently occurs throughout schools and the sporting community.

It would be great if this behavior were eliminated, but unfortunately, it will likely remain for some time.

What does bullying even mean?

A bully will try to make you feel less about yourself.

They will talk down to you and will even talk badly about you to other people.

Why would they do this?

There are many reasons why they attack other people, and it really sucks for the people on the receiving end.

Often, they do this because they want everyone to think they are big, bad, and that nothing bothers them.

It seems like their life's purpose is to make other people miserable.

If you have been bullied, it doesn't feel good.

How do you handle this though?

Oftentimes, bullies don't feel great about themselves. They feel threatened or jealous of how well other people are doing, so they attack and try to bring them down to make themselves feel better.

When you respond to them with anger, they love that.

More commonly, they have something going on inside and that is why they lash out at others.

Try not to take it personally; the words that they say are hurtful, but they come from a place of hurt.

The bully is often hurting on the inside more than anyone will ever know.

ACTION STEPS

1) You have control! Do not let negative words dictate how you feel.

   You do not deserve that.

2) Love not hate!

   They want to see that you are affected negatively. It makes them feel better.

3) Help them! Offer to help. Ask them if they are ok.

   This may be the difference to help them turn their life around!

4) Are you the bully? If you have something on the inside that is really bothering you, talk to someone.

DON'T BE A HATER!

67
STAY IN THE MOMENT

Are you the type of person who always dwells on things?

Do you worry and stress out too much?

If you have trouble staying in the moment, you are likely carrying around too much stress and worry.

When you think of the past and future all the time, stress, worry, and anxiety will be present.

You cannot change what happened in the past and you do not know exactly how the future will play out.

The important takeaway is how you respond to what happened to you in the past. Did you view it as a learning experience or continue to think about and re-live the hurt?

Here's an example:

Late in the game, you started backchecking but could not catch the forward streaking down the ice. You stopped short, and they went on to score the game winner!

Did you just accept that they were faster than you or were you able to view the situation differently?

Was it because your cardio wasn't quite right?

What did you do after that game? Did you decide to get in better shape?

That was the issue, not that the other player was quicker or more talented than you.

Rarely will talent overtake hard work and heart!

Next, are you constantly thinking about the "what if" of the future?

The future will occur either way, but what matters right now is the NOW!

Everything you do in the moment will dictate how the future plays out.

You cannot alter the events in the past, you don't know exactly how the future will play out, but you do have control over how you ACT in the moment!

If your priorities are out of alignment, then you may find your mind wandering in and out of the past.

Keep it simple. What is your big goal?

Identify the daily tasks needed to move you closer to that goal.

When you are working on the task, be there in the present moment and focus 100% on the task at hand.

The past already occurred and the future you are dreaming of will never occur if you don't take care of the present tasks!

Yes, you should visualize your future goals occurring but remember they will not happen without the work ethic!

Stay where your feet are!

ACTION STEPS

1) Do your very best in each moment.

2) Start paying attention to your thoughts. You have thousands of thoughts each day, that will always happen.

   Be aware of how often you are thinking of the past or worrying about the future.

3) Be patient. It will take time to retrain your brain and really

embrace the NOW!

4) Speak up - Your parents are there to help you. Explain to them how you are feeling.

They were once in "kid shoes" too!

BE WHERE YOUR FEET ARE!

68
STOP COMPLAINING

Are you the type of person who complains and blames other people for what is happening?

As human beings, we like things to go our way and can get upset when they don't.

Often, we feel that we have done everything possible and there is no way that it could be our fault.

Ask yourself, did you really do everything possible?

How many times did you try before you stopped?

"But I've tried everything," you say. Really, how many times did you actually try? Once, twice, maybe a handful of times.

Champions complete thousands of repetitions.

Have you done everything possible and left nothing on the table? Be honest!

Don't complain, find the SOLUTION!

Here is an example:

Your goalie let in a goal that you feel they should have handled. So, naturally, people start pointing the finger at the goalie and blame them for the loss.

That is not fair!

That same goalie saved 37 other shots that game. The real question is why the other team was getting so many shots in the first place?

The problem is not your goaltender, it is what happening in front of them.

Is your team playing too loose, too soft?

Stop complaining about the goal and focus on how your team can reduce the number of shots! That's the real issue!

If you want to blow past your potential, it has to get uncomfortable.

Are you challenging yourself physically? If you are underperforming physically, it surely affects how you perform in other areas of your life.

ACTION STEPS

1) Own YOUR STUFF!

    Ensure you put in 100%, that's what matters.

2) Be a problem solver!

    Identify the problem and figure out the solution.

3) Be positive!

    Complaining creates negative energy. We do not perform at peak performance in a negative state of mind. STOP!

4) Get Physical - When you challenge yourself physically, you will overcome tough moments and will build resiliency. The more times you build resiliency, you are building your personal grit factor!

    **Now, when times get tough on the ice, in the classroom, or in your chosen career, your newfound grit will help you bust through the obstacles and not look back!

DON'T BE THE PROBLEM, BE THE SOLUTION!

69
IT'S OK TO BE BORED

Are you bored and just do not know what to do?

Do you resort to wasting time on your phone and just float through the day?

This is not the type of bored we will be focusing on here.

Showing up every day and doing what needs to be done could be the most important factor in your success journey!

If you speak with professional athletes and successful business owners, they all say that you must show up and do the work every day, especially when you do not feel like it!

This sounds like such an easy philosophy, doesn't it?

So, why are there not endless hockey superstars out there?

1) Most people understand what they need to do, but they do not follow through.

2) The people that do the work often get bored and stop.

Yes, this is the "boring" being referred to here!

Once you identify the areas that need improvement, you put your plan in place with the best intentions.

You do the tasks required each day to become a better hockey player.

You are seeing the improvements, you are happy, and everything is moving along nicely, but then you just STOP." WHY?

You get bored and need excitement and stimulation, so you go do something else.

This is human nature, so don't feel bad if this happens.

Here's the takeaway! *Successful people are ok with being bored.*

They understand that completing the tasks each day (even when they don't want to) will help them fully refine the skillset needed to improve!

ACTION STEPS

1) See it through!

   Try not to get "shiny ball syndrome." Once you identify the area that needs improvement, do the tasks needed to ensure you are getting better. Don't quit too early.

2) Smile when bored!

   Most people will start chasing the next "quick fix."

   Stay focused, finish what you started, then re-evaluate what is needed next.

   IT'S NOT ALL FIREWORKS IN THE SKY!

70
WINNERS DON'T MAKE EXCUSES

Do you feel like you should be further ahead?

Do you believe that success should be given to you because you have worked so hard?

When you review parts of your game, you may get upset because you are not the fastest skater, don't have the best shot, or don't have the size of other players.

When you identify the weaknesses in your game, you are taking the first step to becoming successful!

Now, that you've identified the areas that you need to touch up, it's time to plan out how to strengthen them. We have discussed this many times already.

This is the key takeaway.

Even though you put in the many hours, many sets, and reps, you are never guaranteed anything!

Winners do not make excuses when this happens; they keep grinding each day.

Losers quit because it is too difficult, and the results did not happen overnight!

Here is more of the harsh reality.

There will be times when people make fun of you for your dedication towards your dream. This can especially hurt when you fail and fall short.

Are they right, should you stop because all the work and sacrifice is not worth it?

NO. You don't have to prove anything to them.

If you want to live the life of your dreams, you must go to war with yourself.

Identify your weaknesses, seek feedback if needed to overcome them, and begin creating your new identity!

ACTION STEPS

1) Stay in the game! Show up each day and keep doing what needs to be done to improve.

2) Slow is fast! Many people fail because they go for the home run and try to exponentially improve overnight.

   *Start by getting better by 5% in all the important areas of focus.

   i) Workouts - This could be increasing the intensity or duration by 5%.

   ii) Study time - Spend the extra 5% to make sure you fully understand.

   (When do you study? If you are a morning person, it will be easier to focus in that time period)

   iii) Wake up earlier - Don't try to get up an hour earlier right away.

   Get up a few minutes earlier each day to focus on your "most important task."

   The TASKS that are going to move the needle closer to your big goal!

2) Be resilient! Not everything is going to go your way or seem fair.

Assess WHY the result did not occur and get back to work!

CHAMPIONS ARE NOT BUILT OVERNIGHT!

71
KEEP CHIPPING AWAY

When was the last time you gave up way too soon?

When was the last time you completed 100s or 1000s of REPS to improve?

Thomas Edison had over 1000 failed attempts while inventing the light bulb.

Most people will quit after only a few failed attempts.

Remember the story about Sidney Crosby practicing thousands of faceoffs in preparation for the one that counted in the Stanley Cup playoffs!

If you are willing to do the work behind the scenes when others are scrolling on social media, it is only a matter of time before you start surpassing your competition.

When you are doing the extra stickhandling, running, learning from books or videos, you are already doing more than most.

There will be times when you do not feel like it, but you must remind yourself, "If I am not willing to do the REPS, someone is willing!"

Do not leave your success up to chance!

Here is a classic Kobe Bryant example:

Kobe admittedly did many training sessions during each day, year after year.

He explained that if you are focusing on your craft intently and putting in more focused hours than your competition, the results will speak for themselves.

If you are doing this for years, it won't matter if someone decides to work really hard one summer before the season starts.

They will never catch up to you!

ACTION STEPS

1) Outwork them! Other players may be more talented than you, but they cannot outwork you.

2) Question yourself! When you are grinding away and doing the reps, ask yourself

   "Am I doing enough?"

3) Do one more rep! Most people will stop at the prescribed number of reps for that set.

   If you are asked to do 10, do 11!

DO NOT QUIT TOO EARLY!

72
DISCIPLINE NOW

Are you disciplined, day in and day out?

Are you willing to be uncomfortable now to be successful later?

What are you willing to sacrifice to become a better player and continue to grow as a person?

How bad do you want it? Are you happy with being in the same spot each year?

Most of your competition are not willing to be disciplined because it is uncomfortable.

Once you have identified the areas that you need to improve upon, it is really simple after that…JUST SHOW UP!

There will be days that you are tired, not feeling great, and decide to just do it tomorrow. This is the difference between good and excellent.

Champions continue to complete the reps when the conditions are not perfect.

They will grind out a few more drills while others sit on the sidelines.

This greatness that is inside all of you is available and can be tapped into more easily than you think.

No, the work should not be easy, but the available greatness always comes down to YOU!

If you want it bad enough and commit to showing up each day, the sky will be the limit! The majority will not put their full effort in on a daily basis.

Do not be the majority!

ACTION STEPS

1) Gamechanger - Get a workout accountability partner.

   i) This could be someone that you physically work out with each session. You will be more likely to complete the session if you are meeting someone to do it!

   However, this is not always possible.

   ii) Accountability partner through messaging!! It could be a parent, sibling, or friend.

   Simply tell them what you are planning on doing and then message them after you have completed the activity!

   There will be days when you are not feeling like doing the work. Message them for support.

   A great partner will inspire you to get moving and complete the task.

2) Do the work! Keep this as simple as possible. Do the work when you do not feel like it!

   Most people will not do that...use this advantage!

3) SET A BIG GOAL! Set a big goal for yourself and attach an exact date with it.

   Write it down and post it in your training area.

   When you feel like not showing up or completing the training session, look at that goal.

   You have unfinished business to take care of.

   LET'S GO!

   KEEP IT SIMPLE, WORK ON YOURSELF DAILY!

73
OLD SCHOOL ROAD HOCKEY

When was the last time you played road hockey?

Do you feel that your development is contingent upon signing up for an organized training session?

Road hockey is often overlooked these days because there are so many development programs available.

You should choose the right development program for your current needs.

You do not need to do them all!

Road hockey is great for so many reasons.

First, it is fun, and you get to play hockey with your buddies!

It allows you to be creative and try things you cannot do in the organized format of a practice or development session.

It is harder to control a ball, and you will become more proficient and inventive if you incorporate a ball into your skill development.

Here is an example from when I played baseball as a kid.

We decided to play mini-baseball in our backyard. This involved a little mini baseball bat and a ball made up of Kleenex with duct tape wrapped around it.

It was very hard to hit the little ball, but with practice, we got better and were able to make solid contact.

When it was time to return to a regular batter's box, the real baseball looked like a beachball, and we just crushed it!

Road hockey is a fun activity to play with buddies and is an activity overlooked for hockey development.

> ## ACTION STEPS
>
> 1) Be the organizer! If you don't plan it, the game will never happen.
>
>   Start today and organize an old-school road hockey game!
>
> 2) Be creative! You do not have to be serious all the time. Enjoy and embrace the opportunity to be creative. You will be having fun and not even realizing that you are developing your skillset!
>
>   **IF YOU ORGANIZE IT, THEY WILL COME!**

74
BUY A STOPWATCH

Are you currently tracking your progress?

How do you know if you are improving your cardio performance if you do not track it?

Throughout this book, you have learned that nothing is going to be handed to you for free. If you want to improve, there will be work involved, lots of work.

Warriors will do the work. If you have read this far, you have taken the next step to become a savage hockey warrior.

But, how do you know if you have really improved your performance?

There are obvious ways to gauge how you are doing.

Your on-ice performance will be noticeable and results will speak for themselves!

However, how do you know if your cardio performance is improving?

Do not leave it to chance. When you are doing cardio drills, time your sessions.

Keep it simple!! The next time you perform the same drill, aim to knock off a few seconds!

It doesn't have to be a fancy stopwatch, your phone will work.

Time it and track it in a notebook!

ACTION STEPS

1) Just track it! It takes a little more time to track your training sessions, but you will always have the records to ensure you are making progress.

   If you put in all this hard work, you want to make sure you are improving.

2) Start today! Simple, if you don't track it, it didn't happen.

   Be accountable to your success path!

   TRACK YOUR SUCCESS!

75
OLD SCHOOL MINI-HOCKEY

When is the last time you played mini-hockey in the basement?

Mini-hockey is often played by younger kids. It is a lot of fun and an opportunity to be super creative!

Just like road hockey, there are many benefits to this activity.

First, you are playing on a little net, and your shot must be precise to snipe on those little nets. You are stickhandling in close quarters with a ball that is harder to control in comparison to a puck.

When you go on the ice, you are now able to see the ice more clearly and your mini-hockey precision skills are easier to apply on the larger nets.

The most important part is the opportunity to dream and visualize something that has not happened yet.

You have the opportunity to pretend that you are one of the top players or goalies in the league. You pretend that it is Game 7 and the score is 2-2. Next goal wins the Stanley Cup! Be honest, I know you have done this, and if you haven't, you must try it.

When you place yourself in this competitive situation, even though it's not the real Stanley Cup, you are preparing yourself for the real-life hockey games that come down to the wire.

When you visualize and in this case participate in events that you want to happen, the reality of them becoming true is much higher.

You may never play in a Game 7 Stanley Cup, but you have played 100s of Game 7s in your basement.

You will lose some, you will win some, but more importantly your fun, pretend Game 7s will prepare you for when the game is on the line in your league!

ACTION STEPS

1) Organize it! Just like road hockey, you must be the one to begin playing again.

    You will develop the little details and it is FUN!

2) Creatively dream! Put yourself in those make-believe Game 7s and be your favorite player.

    BE WHOEVER YOU WANT TO BE!

76
READ THE COMPETITION

What are you doing when you are waiting on the bench?

Are you just watching the game or are you learning?

Are you watching how the centerman is taking faceoffs?

Are you watching which side is weakest for the defense so you can exploit it?

Are you paying attention to the goaltender's tendencies?

Are you paying attention to each player's tendencies?

Do they always go left?

Do they always shoot high?

Do they cut back into the middle?

This list could go on and on, but the key takeaway is that you must pay attention to these details to understand what the competition is most likely going to do.

NFL quarterbacks study for hours and hours to understand the tendencies of the opposing defenses. They don't just show up and start running random plays and hope they work.

You, too, can operate like an NFL quarterback!

Pay attention when you are on the bench.

This is a tactic that is free, and most will never utilize it.

The competition will be frustrated because it will seem like you know their next move...that's because you do!

ACTION STEPS

1) Be a student! Do not just wait for your next shift.

   Grab a drink of water, take a deep breath, stand up, and learn!

2) Pass it ON! When you learn something unique about the competition, pass along that information to your teammates.

3) Behind the curtain - Your team generally plays the same loop of teams each year.

   Start taking notes on the players on the other teams.

   * Be relentless, learn their tendencies, and shut them down!

ACTIVELY REST AND LEARN ON THE BENCH!

77
PRE-GAMEMOVEMENT

How do you feel when you are in the dressing room?

Are you energized, muscles loose, and ready to go?

What did you do all day at home waiting for your game?

Did you just sit around and relax or did you move around to ensure your muscles were loosened up for game time?

But..won't this activity wear you down before the game?

A friend of mine is a marathon runner, and I asked him how he prepared for a race.

He informed that he ran and stretched before the race. He worked hard enough to generate a sweat and challenge his breathing.

Why would you want to exert that much energy prior to a race?

This also applies to your pre-game preparation.

You are going to battle in the arena, while he is going to battle for 26 miles.

Does your body perform better in a cold, unstretched condition or will you hit your stride earlier if the body is warmed up?

On game days, feel free to go for a light jog, ride a bike, and shoot some pucks.

Fifteen to twenty minutes will be enough to have your body primed and ready for battle!

Next, most teams have fantastic pre-game routines to help warm-up your body and mind.

However, if your pre-game warm-up is too far in advance, your body will retract as you sit in a warm dressing room in your equipment.

One way around this is to conduct the team warm-up closer to your ice time.

You would then come back in the room, get dressed, crank the music, and get pumped for the game.

When there is a limited time lapse between warm-up and puck drop, the body remains loose and there is limited time to get distracted and lose focus.

If you are not mentally and physically prepared prior to jumping on the ice, consider the following:

ACTION STEPS

1) Water intake! Ensure you have consumed lots of water at home before the game, in the dressing room, and on the bench.

    Also, splash water on your face before the game!

2) Move around! Just because your teammates are sitting in the dressing room doesn't mean you can't get up and move around.

    You can get out of the dressing room into the cooler area. Do some stretching and even crush a few jumping jacks to get your blood flowing.

3) Mentally prepare! Sit back with your helmet on and visualize what actions you will be taking on the ice!

    It's so powerful! See it and believe before it even occurs!

4) Go outside! Encourage your trainer to conduct the warm-up

outside.

It will definitely wake you up! Let's GO!

GET UP FOR THE GAME!

78
PROS GO TO WORK

How often do you feel like not doing the work you need to do to improve?

Do you do it anyway or just blow it off until tomorrow?

If you consistently push the difficult tasks off until tomorrow, you are not going to reach the level you are hoping for.

There will be times when your motivation is low. It happens to the best players in the world!

The PROS go to work when they are tired, don't feel well, and when training time is limited.

If you are using the excuse that there is not enough time, you need to give your head a shake. There are so many pockets of time each day that you can utilize to improve your game.

Here is an example of a common school day:

Most classes begin around 9 AM. There is your first opportunity. Work on the area in your game that needs improvement before school.

Even if you do only 12 minutes, that is 1 hour per week on school days.

Typically, most students go to school for 10 months. Your 12 minutes before school translates into an extra 40 hours over that 10-month term.

Think about you how much you can improve with 40 hours of extra focus on your skills, and you haven't even gone to school yet!

When you get home from school is another time pocket.

Pick a skill that needs refining and get to work.

Again, you don't need to spend a crazy amount of time. 10-15 minutes each day, and you just carved out another 40 hours in that 10-month period.

If you are organized and consistent, your gains will keep building on each other.

When you consistently put more time in each day than your opponents, you will surpass the competition.

The sky is the limit if you are willing to have a PRO MINDSET!

ACTION STEPS

1) Identify the skill! Pick a skill that needs improvement.

    Schedule in a few minutes before and after school when your competition is watching TV or scrolling social media!

2) Be consistent! Once you get into the routine, try not to miss any days.

    Once you retract back to poor habits, it will be harder to re-establish the good ones.

THERE IS ENOUGH TIME!

79
DON'T JUST MAINTAIN IT

Are you content with your current success?

Do you feel that there is no more work to do?

Think closely about the last time you worked so hard and were rewarded.

You stood on the podium, held the trophy, and sang "We Are The Champions"!

This is amazing, and you deserve to celebrate all those moments. You poured in hours and hours of sweat and maybe even a few tears!

Now that you are standing at the top of the mountain, what else is there to prove?

You made it, right?

The champions and pros that we have referred to understand that the work is never completed if you want to remain on top of the mountain!

When people reach the top, they often forget the little things that made it possible to climb that mountain.

When you begin to encounter success (and you will if you are consistent each day), you must continue to do the little things that truly matter.

Close your eyes and envision yourself holding that championship trophy.

This is a very proud moment for so many people, but how many things had to occur for this to become reality?

Keep those eyes closed and think about what you had to do each day to become the best version of yourself.

Every day, every week, and every month, wow that list is growing isn't it!

You were a relentless warrior that completed task after task with a domination mindset.

At first, you felt that you were close to reaching your potential, but soon you learned that there were bundles of greatness inside just itching to bust through the surface.

Not every day was easy, and there were moments when you considered quitting, but you inevitably understood that throwing the towel in would hurt much longer than a few moments of despair!

You continue to learn that the body can handle almost anything, and that it's the mind that will be the limiting factor.

Every year, people from all over the world attempt to climb Mount Everest.

The climb itself is 29,031 feet, but the real obstacles are vast throughout the entire climb. To finish and complete the climb is a monumental accomplishment.

Just like you, there were endless hours of preparation before the event occurred.

No one ends up at the top of Everest because of luck.

The next time you feel like you can take a break and just go back to doing the minimum, think about how it feels to be at the top of the mountain.

You can stay up there if you continue to complete the tasks that were required before you reached the peak!

If you lay down and rest for too long, your competition, opponents, and teammates will catch up and take your spot on the podium!

ACTION STEPS

1) Don't forget! Do not forget what you had to do to reach the new levels.

   Continue doing the hard work behind the scenes when no one is watching!

2) Look back to look ahead! When you feel like you have done enough to achieve the higher levels, it does not mean you will stay up there forever.

   Nothing is going to be handed to you.

   Do the tasks that got you there in the first place.

   GROW DON'T MAINTAIN!

80
WON'T ALWAYS BE PRETTY

Does every rep need to be perfect?

Are you frequently critiquing every little detail?

Hold on, haven't we been focusing on how you need to refine your skills and rep after rep to maximize your skillset?

The reality is that many days, it will be challenging to complete those reps.

These days will prove to be the most influential in your growth.

When these uninspiring moments occur, you have two choices:

You either do the work or you don't.

It is very simple math. The more times you say YES to the discomfort, the higher probability that you will achieve greatness!

Oftentimes, you have probably been told to seek comfort because you have earned it. You've worked so hard to get here, so don't feel bad if you take a few days off.

Yes, it is ok to rest, and you absolutely should.

Listen to your body and rest as needed!

But the more times you decide to take the easy road, the more you will be likely to choose the easy path time and time again.

You will build RESILIENCE when you get down and dirty and complete the repetitions when you really don't want to!

The training session may not be pretty, but at least you showed up.

The crazy thing about these days is when you show up with little drive or motivation, it often turns out to be a very effective session!

ACTION STEPS

1) I feel great! On those days that you are just not feeling it, you must flip the switch quickly and get into the zone.

   Simply say "I feel great" 10 times. You will begin to feel the energy enter your body.

   Now, get after it!

2) Your legacy - Review your Big Goal. It will not become reality if you only train when you "feel like it."

3) Battle through it! If you are training and the repetitions are not clean and precise, don't worry about it too much.

   Every day will not be a perfect training session. Keep battling and finish the work.

4) Tell someone - You must have people in your corner who are cheering for you and wish to see you achieve your dreams!

   Who will that be for you? Once you have chosen that person, you must be able to communicate the great moments and the moments when you are questioning the process.

   **On the days when you are considering not doing the work, reach out to your accountability partner to get your head right.

DIRTY REPS ARE BETTER THAN ZERO REPS!

81
KEEP ROLLING

Do you have more winning habits than losing habits?

Is your daily routine organized or do you just wake up and wing it?

Think back to when everything was going great and you were just on fire in all areas of your life.

Wouldn't it be amazing to have momentum on a daily basis, where it all seems to be going your way?

Here is a momentum formula to strive for:

Winning Habits>Winning Routines>Winning Mindsets

We have certainly focused on these many times thus far.

Here's your assignment!

The first part of your assignment is to be self-aware.

When your momentum begins to slow down, you must stop and figure out WHY!

Are poor habits creeping back in?

Is your daily schedule all messed up?

Are you not organized and wasting precious time?

Is your attitude in a positive state or are you becoming too negative?

The KEY here is that you catch it before the *momentum* comes to a screeching halt.

Solid daily habits need to be in place if you want to accomplish your goals.

Habits will come and go, but the ones that mean the most must remain part of your daily arsenal.

Breaking poor habits and instilling newer positive habits will take time, so be persistent and don't give up.

The first obstacle is the three-day mark. Whether you are trying to kick a habit or pick up a new habit, you will find it is difficult to get past the three-day mark.

Next, getting through the 3-4 week barrier is very tough.

There will be instances when everything is going well and then you miss a day or even more. When you miss multiple days, the process to begin that habit again will be very challenging.

Don't give up! Start again and keep showing up daily to fly by the 4-week barrier.

Finally, once you reach the 60-day mark, the habit that you have been so feverishly working to implement is now part of your LIFESTYLE.

It is here to stay and will positively impact your success path.

ACTION STEPS

1) Self-Aware! This is up to you and for you to be honest with yourself.

    Once the momentum slows, you must figure out why.

    *Here is an example -

    Did you miss your training session before school because you didn't wake up in time?

    WHY? It could be as easy as assessing your "lights out" time.

2) Good habits! Focus on incorporating strong habits into your daily routine.

3) Be positive! Winning mindsets have no room for negativity.

   Be kind to others and, more importantly, be nice to yourself.

   You are taking names and kicking butt, you're doing great!

4) Atomic Habits would be a wise book choice!

YOU ARE ON FIRE

82
PAY YOUR DUES

Do you believe that hard work will equal a handout?

Are you working your tail off but getting nothing in return?

Have you heard the stories of athletes making an absurd amount of money for one game, a boxing match, one race or one MMA fight?

There are many instances where athletes have made millions of dollars for one MMA match. When we look at that on the surface, it can be taken out of context.

Believe me, it was not always like this for that athlete.

Everyone must start somewhere!

What we don't see are the thousands of hours that this athlete practiced their craft. All of them had a dream just like you. There was no guarantee.

Actually, there was one guarantee, and that is that their greatness would never have become reality if they did not… pay their dues.

There were times when they were putting their heart and soul into the game and they too had doubts as to whether it was all worth it.

Paying your dues is not just about the hard work. It's about the beginning, the first step that is required. When you take the first step, you have made the choice to go all in on yourself.

It's also about the endless hours spent perfecting your craft, with no guarantees!

It also refers to doing what is right, no matter what, because it's just the right thing to do.

A great example is *volunteering your time for a good cause.*

When is the last time you felt like you didn't have to complete a task because you had already paid your dues? You did the dirty work and now you deserve more respect, don't you?

When is the last time you volunteered for something because you recognized that someone needed help?

When you volunteer for something, you are helping out and leading with value. This is an attribute that will serve well inside and outside the arena.

You sincerely want to help, and nothing is expected in return.

The reward is seeing the elation and joy in the eyes of the recipient.

When you raise your hand and volunteer, you will gain more experience and the coach, parent, or teacher will indeed offer more respect to the people who go above and beyond for them!

These people will be more apt to lend you a hand when your hand is raised!

ACTION STEPS

1) Just begin! On the surface, it may look like it's all sunshine, rainbows, and superstardom.

    But the greats took the first step just like you and suffered heartache all the way to the podium!

2) Raise your hand! The more doors that you open, the more chances you will have for opportunities to learn and improve.

3) Don't forget! Do not ever forget where it all started.

    If you stay in the game long enough, you will improve and be successful.

Always remember all the grinding that was needed to get you there.

4) Thank them! Take time to thank all the people that believed in you and gave you the opportunity.

RENT IS DUE, GO GET IT!

83
TAKE THE CHANCE

Do you wait for things to happen or do you make them happen?

Have you ever been close to giving up because it didn't seem worth it?

A phrase that will prove useful to you is, "There is always a chance."

This simply means that you never know what will happen, but one thing is for sure, if you quit it will *not happen!*

If you don't take the first step, nothing will change!

There will be times when nothing seems right and you begin to lose the belief that it ever will be. This is when you must lift your head high and say "There is always a chance."

If you are willing to endure hard workouts and sweaty practices and do the work when no one is watching, there is always HOPE!

But if you give up too early, that hope, that chance, will darken into the shadows and *your shot* will never become reality.

Think about it this way…if you never take a shot during the game, your team will lose. You will go through the motions all game, but there is no chance to win because you cannot score.

When you get a chance on the ice or off, you must go for it.

Champions are ok with this because they know nothing great will happen if you don't take the chance.

At that moment, you cannot predict what will happen.

Cherish the opportunity that is before you because it may not occur again.

That one opportunity, that one moment, may have been the "difference."

Wayne Gretzky once said, "You miss 100% of the shots you never take."

ACTION STEPS

1) Believe! Keep believing that greatness will happen.

   If you give up that HOPE, you will never reach your potential.

2) There is a chance! When you make the decision to "never give up," there will be more and more chances. You will get knocked down on and off the ice. The important part is how you respond!

3) Take the shot! Nothing great in life will just be handed to you.

   When you have the opportunity on and off the ice, take the shot and see what happens!

DON'T EVER GIVE UP!

84
BELIEVE IN THE END RESULT

Do you believe that all this work will be worth it?

Can you see the end of the path very clearly?

Once you have established that big goal that you want to achieve, you MUST expect it to happen!

You must believe deeply that it is going to happen.

If you start thinking of the ways that it will not occur, you are allowing negative thoughts to enter your mind.

Negative thoughts will affect your performance. If something does not go as planned, getting down on yourself is common.

Is this something that you have done before?

It may not seem like a big deal on the surface. However, when you are constantly critiquing what you did wrong, it impacts your decisions in the future.

You will miss a shot and you will lose many games, that is the reality of sports.

Keep your head high and believe the positive result will occur next time.

Believing down to your core ties in with visualization. When you close your eyes, you see yourself achieving the dream. You see yourself scoring the goal!

You see yourself making the *team!*

You *must* expect it to happen. You must FEEL IT.

Is it safe to say that one of your big goals is to make the NHL?

If you play hockey, this accomplishment has entered your mind.

This is a very audacious goal and only a select few will ever grace the ice on an NHL team!

Here's how you tweak that way of thinking to level-up your training and end results.

When kids are asked, "What do you want to do when you grow up?", they often respond by saying, "I want to play in the NHL."

Playing the NHL would be amazing, but that should not be where it ends.

During your next workout, skill session, or practice, start saying:

"I want to be the best playmaker in the NHL, I want to lead the league in scoring, I want to be on the first line, I want to be on the powerplay unit, and I want to be called upon when the game is on the line."

When you change your mindset to "I must be the best" in specific categories, the approach during your training sessions will be different.

You won't settle for good enough.

See it, believe it, and get to work!

ACTION STEPS

1) Expect it! Close your eyes and see it happening!

    This is not a one-time thing.

    Visualization is a powerful tool but must be done consistently to be effective, and you still have to put in the reps!

2) Positivity! The results will not always be what you envisioned or hoped for.

    Assess why it didn't go well and keep your head high.

Then work on improving the fault.

3) Do the work! One thing is for certain.

If you do not put in the work, the results will not happen!

SEE IT TO BELIEVE IT!

85
BACK TO THE BASICS

Is your technique as good as you think it is?

When is the last time you had your basic skills assessed by someone else?

There has been a lot of focus throughout this book on doing the work and completing the repetitions. If your work ethic is not sound, your dreams will be in jeopardy.

Having the discipline to improve upon your personal standards will help clear the path to continual improvement.

You are getting closer to committing to go all-in and make this happen!

Let's go get it, right?

You have the vision now: you are going to embrace the grind, and no one is going to get in your way! You believe in yourself, you can see the light, and it's time for you to reach greatness!

Perfect, let's get after it and make a difference.

Ok, slow down for just a second.

You are committed to putting in thousands of repetitions, so let's make sure you are doing them properly.

You may not agree with the advice. Push your ego aside and accept the truth.

Your current game is not being attacked or threatened.

The flaws are being assessed right now to refine your future path.

Will you change or deny the truth?

ACTION STEPS

1) Take the lesson! Connect with your coach or the instructor of your program development.

    Have them critique your shooting, passing, and skating technique.

2) Refine them! Perfection will not occur overnight.

    You are committed to doing all these repetitions, so ensure you understand how to do them in the first place.

3) Ask again! After a few months, go for another assessment to see if your skills are refined.

    DO IT RIGHT THE FIRST TIME, EVERY TIME!

86
YOU ARE THE BEST

How do you view yourself?

Do you think you have what it takes?

Yes, this is another mindset-based tactic.

If it was good enough for Michael Jordan, Wayne Gretzky, and Tom Brady, it's in your *best* interest to incorporate this into your daily routine.

You must *believe* you are the best before you are the best!

The mind is a very powerful tool that a lot of people never take advantage of.

If you continue to believe you are the best, you will keep moving towards that status.

Believe it early and throughout your entire journey.

But you cannot become great by just thinking it. There is another ingredient as well, and I think you are well aware what that is.

You will have to work extremely hard to stand beside the greats.

Work hard, believe that you are good enough, and do not let anyone else try to knock you down.

I get it, everyone has told you to work hard, but what does that mean to you?

Hard work is when there is nothing left in your tank and somehow you find a little more. This is not for a week or a month. It is every shift, every practice, every repetition.

Only you know if your personal actions should be defined as hard work!

The results, championships, and trophies will all become reality if you are willing to "never give up."

However, to maintain a relentless, warrior mindset, you must embrace the process.

Striving to improve is a way of life, it's not about the end result.

Once you get to this point, you become unstoppable!

But wait, not everyone will be in your corner, pat you on the back, and truly want the best for you.

A lot of people do not like to see others succeed and may try try to bring you back to their level. It's a shame, but this is reality.

You control the outputs. You control how you react to people, that is your output.

You cannot control what other people say, but you do have control of how you will process it. Be careful of who you choose to be part of your input circle!

ACTION STEPS

1) Say it! Physically begin saying "I am the best" to yourself.

    It is not meant to think you are above everyone, it is meant for you to realize that you can be the best if you believe and do the work!

2) Be careful! Be aware of how other people are speaking to you.

    Are they offering encouragement or trying to hold you back?

    Aim to surround yourself with people that have ambitious dreams like yourself!

YOU'RE THE ONE!

87
IT'S THE LAST 10%

Were you so close but decided to quit?

Do you regret not finishing what you started?

Close your eyes and think of an instance when you worked really hard, made lots of progress, and didn't achieve your goal.

This happens all the time in sports, business, and of course in your school studies.

The majority of society will be able to show up and do *most* of the work.

If the goal was 100%, most people will get to the 90% level. Then it gets nasty and extremely difficult.

They don't feel comfortable anymore and decide to quit.

They will justify in their brains that it is ok to STOP and not continue towards their dreams. It's just not meant to be!

So here is another advantage for you. If most people are not willing to get down and dirty for the last 10%, then you are in a great spot.

It's not that they are not talented enough, they just don't have the courage and commitment. It's cold and lonely in the last 10%, but that's ok because that means you are so close to the *breakthrough!*

When you recognize that times are getting tough and begin questioning whether all this work is worth it, you are so close.

You see, most people don't like feeling this way and they STOP, and that is the end of their dream.

There are no shortcuts. We live in a world where people believe they should get what they want and are entitled to their dream.

If you are willing to get dirty in the last 10%, you will succeed in the arena, in the classroom, and in whatever career you choose.

Be **patient**, your time is coming.

REFUSE to quit! REFUSE to throw in the towel! REFUSE to lose!

ACTION STEPS

1) You don't get tired! Being tired is not an excuse to let your dream slip away.

   You have come too far to only come this far!

   The last 10% is where your greatness will rise!

2) Feel it! When you get to that 90% level, you must feel discomfort.

   Once you have encountered the cold and nasty feeling, you are now aware that the breakthrough is close.

   Don't quit too soon!

   YOU'RE SO CLOSE!

88
SIZE OF THE DOG

Do you feel like you are not built the same as other players?

Are you the smallest player on your team?

If you are not the biggest kid on the team, do not become discouraged.

"It is not the *size* of the dog in the fight, what is most important is the size of the FIGHT inside the dog!"

You may not be the tallest or have the biggest muscles on the team, and that is ok.

It is not healthy to compare your physical attributes to those of others.

This is called comparison syndrome, and social media does not help the situation.

Focus on what you need to do and stop worrying about other people. They have their own issues and skills they need to work on.

When the game is coming down to the wire and every shift could be the difference, it will not be the physical size of the player that dictates the outcome.

The grit, desire, and perseverance inside of YOU will prove to be the most important "muscle" you need!

Compete in every drill and every shift, win every scrimmage, and strive to dominate the competition.

Be like a dog on the bone. Relentless to the point that the opponent retreats because it is apparent that you are never going to let down or give up.

This muscle is your *heart*. The heart is "the size of the fight" inside the dog.

Look around at all the bigger kids on the other team and say to yourself,

"It doesn't matter how big you are, I WILL OUTWORK YOU!"

ACTION STEPS

1) Train your heart! Many people go to the gym to build their body on the outside, but their grit level on the ice stays the same.

   Put yourself in situations that are tough and outside your comfort zone.

   Feel how uncomfortable it is, dig deep, and build that heart muscle.

   You have a choice every time you go to practice and games to build this grit even further.

2) Dare to compare! Do not be intimidated by someone's physical size; it is often an illusion.

   Look at the bigger kids and start believing that your hard work will be the difference.

   You MUST outwork them!

CHALLENGE ACCEPTED!

89
DON'T BE NERVOUS

Are you the type of person who just keeps thinking and worrying about things?

Do you question that you are not good enough and do not belong here?

If you are worrying and cannot turn off your mind, don't stress about it, this is very common.

Oftentimes, when we worry and overanalyze something, it's because we are not prepared. We haven't done the work yet, so we are nervous that we will fail and be embarrassed.

So the simplest answer is, identify what area you need to improve in and do the work! Yes, it is that simple.

Think back to a game or situation where you did not want to be the person taking the last shot or jumping over the boards during overtime battle?

Was it because of fear of failure or fear of embarrassment?

Even the most successful athletes on the planet have missed many game-defining shots. The key was that they had the *courage* to take the shot!

How did they develop that courage to want to be the athlete who takes the game-winning shot every time?

They spent endless hours working on their craft. They completed the repetitions when no was else was watching. Nobody else expected them to or even cared whether they did the workout or not.

They understood that their skills needed continual refinement to gain enough confidence to crave the main event: the final SHOT!

When it came time to play in a championship game or take the game-defining shot, they were not nervous.

There was nothing to be nervous about because there was nothing else they could have done.

They spent thousands of hours practicing to gain that supreme confidence in themselves.

They will not score every shot they take, and they are ok with that.

The reality of sport is there will be a winner and a loser, a game won or a game lost.

The athlete must be comfortable with losing and missing that shot because they know in their heart that they could not have done anything else behind the scenes!

ACTION STEPS

1) Do the work! At the end of the day, only you know whether you put in your full 100% effort.

    Look in the mirror at the end of the day and ask yourself, "Did I put in 100% effort today?"

    Be honest and call yourself out if you didn't!

2) Take the shot! You must want to take that shot. You won't score every time, but you will never score if you do not take any shots!

    Don't be nervous because you know that what you did behind the scenes was your true 100% effort level!

    ONLY YOU KNOW!

90
YOU HAVE CONTROL

How has your hockey life been affected by COVID-19?

Has it become stronger or weaker because of it?

In the spring of 2020, we encountered a global pandemic when the virus COVID-19 spread throughout the world.

Schools closed, businesses shut down, and all sports came to a screeching halt!

Most kids did not have the opportunity to play hockey for many months.

I think we can agree that this was a scary time and certainly frustrating in so many ways.

You were playing hockey multiple times each week, and boom! Just like that, no more hockey for months.

How did you handle this adversity?

What did you do during the lockdown to improve and become a better person?

Sure, it was a stressful situation and very difficult for a young child to comprehend.

You were locked down and confined to your home.

Look yourself in the mirror (again, I know…) and ask, "Did I improve or retract during the COVID-19 pandemic?"

Day after day, there were many hours that could have been used to *improve yourself*.

The point is, COVID or something else, you have control over what you do with the hours available each day.

It is very unfortunate that you worked so hard all year and didn't even get to try out for the team that you wanted to make.

However, life isn't fair and will continue to challenge what is right and wrong.

The key is how you will respond to the adversity. Will you let others knock you down and keep you down?

It is totally normal to get knocked down.

The question is, how will you respond?

Will you get up, dust yourself off, and set another goal?

If you've read this far, the word "quit" is not going to be part of your vocabulary anymore!

ACTION STEPS

1) Get up! There will be many times in your life when it will seem unfair and people are against you.

    Life will happen in many seasons, some are going amazing and then all of a sudden, the rug is pulled right out from under you.

    When you get knocked down, get up and stay in the game!

2) Thick skin! When COVID happened, a lot of people did not handle it very well.

    That is totally ok, as it was a very stressful time.

    But at some point, a personal decision needed to be made.

    Will I do nothing with all this new found time or will I use it to improve?

    Moving forward, be aware of how you are utilizing your time!

USE YOUR TIME WISELY!

91
ARE YOU SCARED TO SUCCEED?

Can you remember the last instance when you gave up?

Have you ever been afraid of the unknown?

One thing that crushes people's dreams every day is fear!

Many people are aware of the fear of failure. Sometimes we do not take chances because we don't want to fail.

On the other side of failure is growth. To excel and move to unknown levels, failure needs to be part of your journey.

Fail early in your life and continue to fail throughout your life.

You will learn the most when the conditions are not nice and cozy.

It will not feel great in the moment, but the long-term gain will be worth it.

Another form of fear is the fear of embarrassment. Generally, human beings do not like to look silly or stupid in front of other people.

This leads to inaction and limited growth because they never take the chance out of fear of looking bad.

Another form of fear, probably lesser known, is the fear of success.

Think back to a time when you were doing very well, making progress, and totally ready to jump into the next level of growth.

Then you just stopped. Why?

Many people are afraid of what is on the other side, even if it is the side of success.

It is unknown, so we retract and go back to the areas where we are comfortable.

The brain likes to protect us and keep us in the place of comfort so we do not get hurt.

Why have you read this far? At the end of the day, you want to excel, become better, and accomplish your personal goals.

Fear of success often occurs because of an event that occurred earlier in life.

Have you achieved something and it wasn't really what you expected or even painful in some way?

It may not even be fear of success, it may be fear of the consequences of that success.

What will my "new normal" be like, will I fit in, and what do I have to do to maintain this?

Sounds stressful, and it certainly can be if you lose track of the simple, bigger picture.

In life, we make many choices during each day. Sometimes our decisions do not align with our values, and we begin to question the process.

To simplify your process, begin asking yourself three questions each day:

i) Who did I help today?

ii) Who helped me today?

iii) What did I learn today?

Leading with value and caring about others' dreams is very honorable.

The more you give in life, the more you receive!

Seeking out advice, feedback, and information will ensure that you consistently improve each and every day.

Keep it simple... help other people and seek help from other people!

ACTION STEPS

1) Go to the other side - Why would you work endless hours towards your goal if you didn't want to reap the rewards?

    If you don't like the newfound success, you can always go back to where you were before.

2) Get over it! Everyone in this world has their own issues.

    Stop worrying so much what other people think.

    They really are not worrying about your failures as much as you may think.

    They have enough personal issues to deal with.

3) Get used to it! Do something that is outside your comfort zone and may be a little embarrassing.

    Once you get used to just being yourself in front of other people, the fear of embarrassment will subside.

    When you become comfortable in your own skin, great things will happen!

BE FEARLESS!

92
FANCY FOOTWORK

How many sports do you play other than hockey?

Would you consider yourself to have quick feet?

The hockey world has put you in a tough situation. There are endless hockey development programs available.

When you look around, it appears that all your friends and certainly your competition are participating in these programs.

There is nothing wrong with personal development, and these programs have so much value within them.

However, are you playing hockey and hockey only?

Do you play hockey all winter (and sprinkle in development) and then continue playing all summer?

You may be thinking, "I will fall behind if I stop playing year round"?

There are many pro players that are advising that you take a break and play other sports. This will help you prevent overuse injuries and "one sport burnout."

What other sports do you enjoy?

Is it soccer, lacrosse, running, swimming or baseball?

All these sports require different skillsets.

They will help improve your footwork, your fine motor skills, hand-eye coordination, and certainly your cardiovascular outputs.

What is the number #1 reason we play any sport in the first place?

I hope your answer is to "Have FUN!"

Think about it this way…are you willing to never kick a soccer ball, throw a baseball or lacrosse ball, or jump off a diving board because you believe that you need to be on the ice year round?

You are only a kid once.

Do not limit yourself to one activity. You are missing out, and you deserve to have more experiences!

Sure, you can still play lots of hockey but branch out and try other things too!

ACTION STEPS

1) Other sports! If you are playing other sports, good for you!

   What other sports interest you?

   Sign up and just go for it!

2) But they do it! By now, I hope you have caught on that the tactics in this book are not what "everyone else" is doing.

   Be yourself and enjoy all the activities that you love!

   MULTI-SPORT ATHLETE!

93
HILL TIME

Are you in great cardiovascular shape?

Do you consider yourself to have powerful, explosive legs?

What muscles would you consider to be the most important to be a strong hockey player?

What muscles are you using the most?

Your *legs* are the base to where everything begins.

Your legs provide power, strength, and agility to allow you to blow by your competition.

You will develop these muscles playing hockey, but there are certainly other exercises available to build those sticks into tree trunks!

Have you ever tried running up a hill?

If you have, you understand that it is not easy. Your lungs and legs are burning, and you may just want to quit.

You may agree that it is difficult to simulate hockey activity.

There is something to say about being in "hockey shape."

Hill sprinting is an activity that is close to that hockey cardio feeling!

You can walk, run, or sprint up the hill. You can even go sideways and perform agility drills. The hill is such a great tracking device.

Each time you go back, you can go a little faster, a little longer, do more sets, do more time, and more effort.

In the end, you can continually track your performance and aim to improve each day you step foot on that hill!

This is another *free activity* that will add another tool into your hockey tool box.

It will take your legs to the next level.

Don't worry, you will have lots of space while training on the hill.

It is a difficult activity, and most people are just not aware of how effective hill training is.

That is why you should schedule in hill training and fly by your competition!

ACTION STEPS

1) Find the hill! Head out into your community and find a few hills.

   Get started! Hill training is going to change your hockey life forever!

2) Go to the woods! Try to find a hill that is situated in the woods.

   You can walk, run, or sprint, it doesn't matter, just be consistent.

   Once you get the hang of it, start choosing trees that you are going to deke around.

   The tree is your competition. Run towards the competition, make a move, and explode around them!

CONQUER THE UNKNOWN!

94
GRAB A PIECE A PAPER

Have you identified your "why"?

It has been mentioned multiple times thus far, and I want to make sure that you are very clear on what your personal WHY is.

If you are not, the probability of success is going to decrease because what are you really striving to accomplish? You don't even know!

Are you clear on your virtues and values?

Some people will go through their entire lives and not understand what their purpose is on this planet.

This is a little exercise that is not physical but is so important in relation to your growth on and off the ice.

Grab a piece of paper and write down your "why."

Write down the first thing that comes to your mind.

Then ask yourself again and again, "What is my why?"

If you ask it more than once, it will help you get deeper into your purpose, not just what you may want on the surface.

Ask yourself "why" multiple times to determine what your real purpose is.

I'll give you a hint, it is more than just becoming a better hockey player!

This technique will also help you achieve breakthroughs in all areas in your life.

There will be many moments when you must ask yourself "WHY."

Why am I not achieving high school grades?

Why am I not improving as a hockey player when I work so hard?

Why am I not connecting with other people?

It is not enough to just ask "why" once, keep asking yourself, and it will help you get to the root of the issue.

Here are a few examples of honorable WHYs!

i) I will never quit, no matter what I am focusing on.

ii) I will be supportive and kind to everyone in my life.

iii) I will outwork the competition, no matter what.

iv) I will go all in for my teammates. Together Everyone Achieves More!

ACTION STEPS

1) Grab a piece of paper! It's time to figure out what your life purpose is.

    Write it down and then start asking yourself "WHY" many times.

    It's ok if you cross out your original answer.

    It is advised that you do this exercise a few times each year.

2) Don't settle! Do not settle for normal or status quo.

    Once you establish your life purpose, go for it.

    Be kind and lead with value, and you will stay on the right track!

    KEEP ASKING!

95
YOU NEED A BREAK

Do you take breaks when you work out or when you are dialed in on an assignment?

Have you ever heard of the Pomodoro Technique?

Human beings can only focus 100% on a task for so long before they begin to get distracted.

Most people can only focus deeply for 20-25 minutes, and then the mind begins to wander.

Especially these days with multiple stimuli that are literally at your fingertips!

The Pomodoro Technique is when you choose a task and work on it for 25 minutes, and then you take a 5-minute break.

The 25-minute period is on a timer!

This is totally relatable to sports.

When the scoreboard timer is winding down and the period is coming to an end, there is a sense of urgency, especially if your team is not winning.

There is only so much time in a game to make a difference.

Your brain is already wired to the stopwatch. It knows that if you do not make something happen when that time clock diminishes, your team will lose!

Now, when you are practicing a skill or working on a school assignment, set the timer and get to work!

Here is an example:

Let's choose stickhandling as the skill that needs refinement.

Fire up the Google and choose a few drills from the references at the back of the book.

Set up the necessary drill station and get ready to go.

Then, set your phone to 25 minutes.

Now, you are to do these stickhandling drills for 25 minutes straight.

Boom, your timer goes off, and it's time to take a 5-minute break.

Choose another skill to improve or a homework assignment that you need to complete, and set that timer to 25 minutes!

ACTION STEPS

1) No distractions! When you are in the 25-minute work period, do not check a text.

   You have work to do, so stay on task for the entire 25 minutes, then take your 5-minute break.

   You will be amazed what you can get accomplished in 25 minutes of non-interrupted work time!

2) Try it! You may be wondering, "How much work am I supposed to complete in that work period?" Once you try it many times, you will have a better understanding of how much work you can complete in this time period.

   The key is that you will complete much more focused work because the distractions are limited and you are dialed in!

THE PHONE IS A TOOL!

96
IT GOES BOTH WAYS

Are you able to drive past the competition on your backhand or forehand?

Do you spend more time working on your wrist shot and slapshot but little time on the backhand?

Are you able to pivot both ways and shut down the driving forward?

Is your blocker side as refined as your glove hand?

Let's be honest, this is probably the reality with most hockey players.

It is more fun to wire a clapper than backhand sauce a pass to a teammate.

It's more fun to make a prolific glove save than guide the puck into the corner with a blocker.

It is more fun to step up on D and make a big hit, but limiting space and guiding a forward into the corner is more beneficial.

Let's use another Crosby example, but make sure you relate this skill to what you must improve in your job role.

Fine-tuning your backhand skills will lead to many more opportunities than the huge windup clapper will!

Who has the best backhand shot in the league?

If you guessed Sidney Crosby, you are *correct!*

His backhand is likely more powerful than many of your forehand shots.

However, it was not always like this. He has spent countless hours working on his shot.

He worked on refining the backhand sauce pass so when a defenseman is gunning him down, it's second nature to gently lift the puck off the ice and over their stick to a charging forward and snipe the game-winner!

When he is in tight with limited real estate, he is able to quickly bury it top-shelf.

So, be honest with yourself and assess your backhand skills.

Is your backhand as proficient as your forehand?

Can you drive the net with efficiency both ways?

Can you pivot effectively in both directions?

Can you slide across the crease both sides equally?

ACTION STEPS

1) Put in the reps! The most efficient way to improve your deficiencies is to simply complete the repetitions and lots of them!

2) Pick up a basketball! Practice dribbling with both hands and driving the hoop with your left and right hands.

   This helps with your fine motor skills and refines your footwork.

   I hope you can agree that hockey is jam-packed with fine skills and footwork!

FIRE AWAY!

97
STOP JAW JACKING

Do you talk a big game but don't show up when it counts?

Do your actions match your mouth?

It is easier to say that you will do something than actually do it!

How many times have you planned to stickhandle, take your 100 shots, crush your push-ups, and finish your HOMEWORK, but you didn't do it?

Here is a quick tip:

Finish your most important work early in the day.

This will be the task that you determine to be the one that improves your game the most.

No one can ever take that away from you. Even if the day gets away from you and no other skills are refined, that's ok because you showed up early and completed the one that mattered the most.

Do not leave your development up to chance!

Finally, do not tell the world every little thing that you are doing.

When people know every little movement that you are making, it can actually backfire on you.

They may now get too involved and interfere with your progress.

They may think there is a better way and start telling you how and what you should be working on.

They may even try to sabotage your big dreams. They do this because they are not happy with their progress, so they like to bring others back to their level.

You can tell people a few things because this does help keep you accountable to what you said you were going to do.

Never give away all of your tricks and ideas to those who you do not have full trust in!

ACTION STEPS

1) Level up! Put your money where your mouth is and do what you said you are going to do.

   Take self-ownership and see it through.

2) Behind the scenes! This is where the magic happens. This is where you grow and improve when no one is watching.

   Nobody else needs to know what extra work you are doing to become a better person.

   You know all the hours that you showed up, and that is what matters!

   GET REAL JACKED!

98
YOU DON'T NEED 10 MOVES

How many go-to moves do you really need?

Are you getting "analysis paralysis" and feeling you need to master many moves?

You will become a more feared opponent if you have a few monumental moves than a bunch of average moves.

No, this does not mean that you don't need to refine your skills in every area of the hockey spectrum.

This is something different, and it will change your game forever.

You need to absolutely master the basics of the game, and that will serve you well throughout your hockey career.

Now, onto the gamechanger!

All the greats have "their moves," the ones that they have worked on for thousands of hours.

When you practice something 1000 times, it will happen naturally without even thinking about it.

What are your best two moves?

First, ask yourself if they are truly effective and help create chances for yourself and your teammates?

Maybe the reason they are not effective yet is because you have not spent enough time dialing them in even further.

Keep going and get dirty mastering your move!

Refine it so much that the competition will have no chance.

Everyone knows that Ovechkin is going to shoot from his office and the goalie still has trouble stopping it!

> ## ACTION STEPS
>
> 1) Narrow it down! You will need to be honest with yourself and identify your top moves.
>
>   Then, make sure that these are the right moves to begin mastering to make an impact.
>
> 2) Strengthen up! You will become a better hockey player and person if you strengthen your weaknesses. We have spent a lot of time discussing this thus far.
>
>   Just think how amazing your best moves will become if you spend more time mastering them even further!
>
> **WHAT'S YOUR NEXT MOVE?**

99
CLIMB THE MOUNTAIN

How often do you feel overwhelmed?

Do you get confused on what task you should be focusing on?

Many people make it more difficult than it really needs to be.

We focus too much on the future, and this makes the end goal feel too far out of reach.

When you look too far ahead, you begin over-thinking all the tasks that are required to achieve that result.

You begin to experience an overwhelming feeling that can come crashing down onto your shoulders.

This is your last lesson, and if you have read this far, your future greatness is much closer than you believe!

I wish I could be on all the journeys that you will go on, and encounter all the hills and valleys with you, but that will not be possible.

The most important person in your journey is YOU!

It's time to climb that mountain!

If you are always focusing on the peak of the mountain, you will miss out on the entire climb.

When you are climbing that mountain, each tree that you encounter is a goal, an obstacle, an opportunity to learn and embrace.

When you feel like you are getting overwhelmed, pick the next tree on the mountain.

Just focus on getting to that next tree. Do not look ten trees ahead because this is too stressful and overwhelming.

Embrace every moment of the journey because oftentimes when we get to the peak, it is not exactly as we envisioned.

If you focus too much on the peak, you truly miss out on each tree. That is what is important.

Get deep into your journey of life.

Embrace it, enjoy it, and get after it!

ACTION STEPS

1) Identify your peak! You must identify where you want to end up so you know to start!

   Keep visualizing that you will achieve that greatness!

2) The trees! Try to stay grounded and not look too far up to the peak.

   Focus on the next tree ahead of you, and embrace the success and failures along the way.

   You will get knocked down many times during your climb.

   Get up, shake it off, and get to that next tree!

IT'S YOUR TIME!

100
THE REWARD

Are you ok with being the exact same person six months from now?

I don't want you to be exactly the same.

I truly want the best for you and would love for you to excel on whatever path you choose in life!

Realistically, WHY did you buy this book and read all the way to the end?

You wanted to improve your hockey game and become a better person, right?

Imagine yourself 6 months from now. You wake up and look in the mirror and smile because you don't even recognize the person from six months ago!

You have become a leader on and off the ice.

You have developed confidence to tackle all obstacles in your way.

Your consistent action taking has catapulted you past the competition.

People are looking to you for guidance and shocked at what you can do.

They initially may not understand your *burning desire* but they are ready to listen.

You have become so relentless and are now ready to conquer all your dreams.

Now, imagine yourself six months from now......

Time to get after it!

ACTION STEPS

1) It's Ok to be Different - Focus on your path and your dreams. Use other people's experiences as guidance, not re-creating their realities.

2) Get Started - You don't need to have everything figured out.

   What is your BIG GOAL. Start today, show up every day and make adjustments along the way!

3) Don't Quit - Some days will be great, some will not.

   Stay focused, be consistent and whatever you do, NEVER QUIT on yourself and your dream!

GO GET YOUR REWARD

Conclusion

SO HERE WE ARE.

Despite me telling you that you didn't have to finish reading this book, you did.

That says something very important about who you are right now and who you will become.

You are a finisher.

You are determined.

You have the grit.

You want better for yourself.

You believe you are destined for more.

And not only that, there are people around you who believe in you.

As much as you may think or feel that sometimes the things you do to improve your future go unnoticed, they don't.

Every visualization of you scoring the winning goal or making the big save before you fall asleep.

Every piece of garbage you pick up when you walk to school.

Every door you open for a stranger.

Every time you stand up for someone who can't stand up for themselves.

Every time you do something to make someone else's life better.

People notice.

They may not always tell you that they believe in you. They may not always go out of their way to give you some encouraging words. But secretly, they admire what you do. They want you to succeed.

I want you to succeed.

And what you have shown with the simple action of reading through this book is that you CAN succeed.

Maybe most importantly is that your success will unlock doors for other people's success IF you stay on your path.

Now, before you close this book for good and move onto whatever is next in your fantastic life…I have one last piece of advice for you.

Dreams do not come true because you "hope" they will.

Your dreams will come true when you decide to MAKE them true.

Let me be clear…this does not mean you have to work your face off every day for the rest of your life.

What MAKING your dream come true means is that you cannot just wait for "the right time."

You can't wait. You can't just dream. You have to do it.

THE END.

Bonus

HOW TO PLAN YOUR PERFECT DAY

PERFECT DAY SCRIPT

DATE

TIME SLOTS

☐ AM/PM
☐ AM/PM
☐ AM/PM
☐ AM/PM
☐ AM/PM
☐ AM/PM
☐ AM/PM
☐ AM/PM
☐ AM/PM
☐ AM/PM
☐ AM/PM
☐ AM/PM

MOST IMPORTANT TASKS TODAY

OTHER TASKS & NOTES

BRAIN DUMP

All Content ©Copyright Early To Rise. All rights reserved

Visit our website at: www.perfectcityformula.com

1) THE NIGHT BEFORE BRAIN DUMP

Your Perfect Day begins the day before.

Each day we have thousands of thoughts that enter our heads. We can become easily overwhelmed if we don't clear our minds.

This will help reduce your stress level because now you can see exactly what needs to be taken care of.

THE BRAIN DUMP

Take a few minutes and write down anything that is on your mind. This would include the skills and areas that you currently working on to improve yourself. It could include assignments that are due in school. It could include upcoming hockey activities. It could also include your current mindset...are you stressed, are you feeling great?

Here is an example:

1) Math Test on Friday

2) Need to Ask my teacher about the Writing assignment

3) Working on backhand in close shots

4) Cardio work needed

5) Hang out with friends

6) Guitar Lesson

7) Need to ask Coach questions about my responsibilities

8) Big game on Saturday

After you have written down all the things that are in your head, take a few moments and put them in order of importance. This means that #1 is the most important item on your list and then position the other items below that. I have already organized the *above items* in terms of importance.

TIME TO PLAN YOUR DAY

Planning your day occurs the day before. Once the brain dump is complete, it will only take a few more minutes to plan your Perfect Day.

Pull out your Perfect Day Planning Sheet and let's get started.

It's time to set your day up for success by scheduling in your Most Important Brain Dump Items.

HOW TO PLAN YOUR DAY (Keep in mind you are creating your Perfect Day Schedule the day before!!)

You must make sure that your most important items are scheduled in FIRST. If you do not focus on the items that are most important to you, your happiness and personal growth will suffer.

1) For simplicity, you can block out 0900am-4pm for your school day.

2) What are you currently doing before school begins? What time do you get up?

Are you sleeping until the last moment and then reaching for phone to check social media?

***Here is a more effective approach that you help you leave your competition in the dust!!

#1 Item is your Math Test, so spend 15 minutes studying before you head out to school.

#3 Item is working on Hockey Development, so you can also do 15 minutes before school.

Instead of rolling out of bed with no plan, you have now focused on your big test and making hockey improvements.

You will still have to time to eat a healthy breakfast and spend a few minutes on social media if you choose.

3) School Time: 0900am-4pm

#2 Item was to ask your teacher about the writing assignment, so schedule it in when others are going out for recess. It will only take a few minutes and now you will be crystal clear on what is needed to complete your assignment.

4) Home From School

Instead of grabbing that phone or video game controller, let's continue to focus on your most important tasks.

#1 Math Test- Study an additional 30 minutes in preparation for you're the math test.

#2- Work on your backhand skills for 15 minutes

#4- Complete Cardio workout

This brings you into dinner time. Instead of wasting time on your device, you have *prepared for your test, improved the area of hockey focus and improved your conditioning.*

People that plan are more productive and will in turn have more time!!

5) Dinner Time 5pm-530pm

6) After dinner you will have lots of time to hang out with friends and participate in other areas that you are passionate about.

If there is more work to do for school, schedule that in right after dinner.

7) If not, have some fun with your friends, go to that guitar lesson, practice another skill, spend some more time studying.

Because you took a few minutes the day before to plan your day, there will be more time available the next day!

**This is because there will be less time wasted.

WHY would you not want to have more time to enjoy all the things you love to do!!

EXAMPLE OF YOUR PERFECT DAY

0700am-Wake Up

0715am-Hockey Skills (15 minutes)

0730-Study for Math Test (15 minutes)

0745-0830- Healthy Breakfast and Surf Phone for a few minutes

900am-4pm- School Time

4pm- Hockey Skills (15 minutes)

415-445pm- Math Preparation

445-5pm- Cardio Workout

5pm-530pm- Dinner Time

530-630- School Work

630- Time to be with friends, Participate in other nonhockey passionate areas

Bedtime- Try to go to bed at the same time each night because your body thrives off of *routine.*

Lights OUT between 830-9pm will ensure you get enough rest to jump out of bed at 7am the next morning to conquer your Most Important Tasks!

Thank you to Craig Ballantyne for providing the Perfect Day Script and the strategies above that will help you build your Perfect Day!

Craig is a world renowned business coach and author of *The Perfect Day Formula, The Perfect Week Formula* and *Unstoppable*.

He is a dedicated, supportive coach who truly cares for his clients.

CraigBallantyne.com

PERSONAL DEVELOPMENT TRAINING RESOURCES

Check Them Out!

NEVER STOP LEARNING!!

YOUTUBE VIDEOS

1) *I Am A Champion-* The Greatest Speech Ever
   https://www.youtube.com/watch?v=yX39j_YyKbs
   You deserve to be a champion in whatever life path you choose!

2) *Sidney Crosby Training*—Motivation- Mentality Of A Winner
   https://www.youtube.com/watch?v=VHvZW6fXiIo

3) *Wayne Gretzky-* Life Changing Advice
   https://www.youtube.com/watch?v=Gjmu0ogcm7M

4) *The Mindset Of A Winner-* Kobe Bryant's Champions Advice
   https://www.youtube.com/watch?v=VSceuiPBpxY&t=53s

5) *Navy Seal Speech-* University of Texas at Austin Commencement Address
   By Admiral William H. McRaven https://www.youtube.com/watch?v=pxBQLFLei70&t=57s

6) *Denzel Washington's Life Advice Will Leave You Speechless*
   youtube.com/watch?v=e3FfL46OzYl
   Believe in yourself and whatever you do, never quit!

7) *The I Am Affirmations-* By Ray Lewis
   https://www.youtube.com/watch?v=xQDvSkgKwEY

8) *The Mindset Of A Champion-* By Carson ByBlow (An 8 Year Old!)
   https://www.youtube.com/watch?v=px9CzSZsa0Y

OFF-ICE TRAINING PLAYER DEVELOPMENT RESOURCES

1) Hockey Canada
   https://cdn.hockeycanada.ca/hockey-canada/Hockey-Programs/Players/Downloads/2018/off-ice-hockey-train-ing-manual-level-1-e.pdf
   https://www.hockeycanada.ca/en-ca/hockey-programs/players/essentials/positions-skills/off-ice

2) Hockey USA
   https://www.usahockey.com/dryland

BOOKS

1) *Make Your Bed: Little Things That Can Change Your Life.... And Maybe The World*, by William H. McRaven

2) *The Perfect Day Formula: How to Own the Day and Control Your Life*, by Craig Ballantyne
   FREE PDF - https://www.freeperfectdaybook.com/giveaway/

3) *The Perfect Week Formula: Build Your Business Around Your Life, Not Your Life Around Your Business*, by Craig Ballantyne
   FREE PDF - https://freeperfectweekformula.com/giveaway

> "Everything you do takes you closer to
> or further away from your goals."
>
> Craig Ballantyne
> *The World's Most Disciplined Man*
> *Business Coach and Author*
>
> CraigBallantyne.com

4) *Coach to Coach: An Empowering Story About How to Be A Great*

Leader, by Martin Rooney

Manufactured by Amazon.ca
Bolton, ON